IN ABSOLUTE
CONFIDENCE

D0851635

The purpose of the Anvil Series is to push back the frontiers of Adventist thought, to stimulate constructive reevaluation of traditional thought patterns, and to catalyze fresh ideas. The concepts presented in the Anvil Series are not necessarily official pronouncements of the Seventh-day Adventist Church nor reflections of the editorial opinion of Southern Publishing Association.

IN ABSOLUTE CONFIDENCE

The Book of Hebrews Speaks to Our Day

William G. Johnsson

Southern Publishing Association, Nashville, Tennessee

Copyright © 1979 by
Southern Publishing Association

This book was
Edited by Gerald Wheeler
Designed by Dean Tucker
Cover design by Bob Redden
Cover Photo by H. Armstrong Roberts

Type set: 11/12 Optima

Printed in U.S.A.

Library of Congress Cataloging in Publication Data

Johnsson, William G   1934-
    In absolute confidence.

    Includes bibliographical references.
    1. Bible.   N.T. Hebrews—Criticism, interpretation, etc.
I. Title.
BS2775.2.J63   227'.87'06   79-1387
ISBN 0-8127-0225-5

DEDICATION

To Terry and Julie
for all the years

CONTENTS

PREFACE

The Book of Hebrews is a marvel and a mystery. The majesty of language, the breadth of ideas, the stately flow of argument—at once we sense that we stand in the presence of a master writer. And yet the concepts are difficult. In it we read of priests and temples, of blood and sacrifices. We hear deep-throated warnings of sins beyond repentance. Afterward we leave with a sense of awe at this enigmatic writing.

Small wonder, then, that Hebrews is a neglected part of the New Testament. Throughout the twentieth century, Protestant scholars of the Word have directed their energies to probing the acknowledged Pauline letters and the Gospels. Hebrews, with its magnificent but remote reasoning, has seemed ever more foreign to the modern Western mind, and scholarship has almost completely bypassed it. Only in the past few years have we seen new evidence of interest in Hebrews, and that is still comparatively slight. Roman Catholic scholars, on the other hand, have shown a continuing regard for the document. Apparently they have felt more at home with the language of priests and sacrifices. Often in their studies we find efforts to discover references to the Mass in Hebrews.

I have been fascinated by the Book of Hebrews for many years. The difficulty of the language (students of the Greek New Testament, rejoicing in mastery of the Johannine literature, find themselves stunned at their ignorance when they turn to Hebrews) and the measured convolutions of argument have drawn me back to Hebrews over and over for nearly twenty years. Out of my study several convictions have sprung up and taken root.

First, if we are to grasp the book, we must understand it as a *whole*. More and more I am convinced of and amazed at the finely honed structure of Hebrews. It is not written piecemeal but as a literary and logical unity, each of whose parts contributes to, and is necessary to, the overall symmetry and progression of ideas.

And herein lies a major criticism of recent studies. They have focused on one part here, another there, a third elsewhere. We have had examinations of the heavenly sanctuary and liturgy, the "rest," the Melchizedek idea, the wandering motif, the eschatology. But while scholars have done much good work, they leave us with a disjointed, even self-contradictory Hebrews. And to say this is to charge students of Hebrews with colossal failure in their efforts to see Hebrews holistically.

Second, I am convinced that Hebrews is not the enigma that we usually think. We may be certain that the pamphlet's author wrote it *to be understood* in its own day—and not just by professors of New Testament! The early Christians did not include many learned and educated men (see 1 Corinthians 1:26-28), yet Hebrews was aimed at them. Indeed, as we shall see in chapter 1, the book has a practical purpose—a point often missed by those who lose themselves in its theological thickets. And we may be confident, I think, that the early Christians understood it.

The modern believer may also grasp Hebrews. The document will not yield its message easily, however. Its closely knit reasoning calls for a degree of concentration that we are less used to than our forebears were. The modern age with its Madison Avenue veneer has dulled our powers. And we must be prepared to *listen* to the writer. In practice that is the hardest part of Bible study. We continually inject our own conceptions into the text. With Hebrews our fault becomes doubly bad, since the book's ideas are so unlike current conceptions or other parts of the New Testament. Only as we sit back and let Hebrews open to us its message in its own terms can we understand it. But then we may indeed grasp it—in its wholeness.

Third, Hebrews *needs* to be understood. The Word of God according to Hebrews has not been heard in its clarity. We have had only dark mutterings, mysterious mumbo jumbo from an age long dead, discordant chords, missed entries, off-pitch melodies. The very neglect of Hebrews by scholars, its shrugging off by even serious lay people, is tragic, *for Hebrews speaks a message for modern Christians*. We shall find in the opening chapter that the problems of the Christians addressed in Hebrews are remarkably similar to those we encounter. Surely we need to hear the solution that the apostle worked out. And without thinking ill of the efforts of our Roman Catholic friends to understand Hebrews, we may add that its message is a distinctly *Protestant* one.

This book is the flowering of these convictions. While I have prepared it in view of the many and various commentaries and monographs on Hebrews, the arrangement and interpretation are mine (Expositors of Hebrews and I, of course, do share many points of common agreement). I have especially drawn upon the work done in my doctoral dissertation, *Defilement and Purgation in the Book of Hebrews*, and subsequent writing and teaching about Hebrews.

The purpose of the work, then, is a basic one: to set out clearly the "message" of Hebrews and to show its significance for Christians living today. I would hope that, while my colleagues in New Testament scholarship could enjoy the work, it would be sufficiently simple in presentation and uncluttered with learned paraphernalia that the minister or layman who loves his Bible may read it with profit.

In Absolute Confidence is not a commentary. Rather, I have sought to isolate the leading ideas of the book and to indicate how they unite in the marvel that is Hebrews. Marvel—and, I would hope, no longer mystery.

William G. Johnsson
Andrews University
Berrien Springs, Michigan

Chapter 1

The "Hebrews" and Their "Letter"

In this chapter we shall seek for a bird's-eye view of Hebrews. Who were the "Hebrews" addressed in the book? What sort of "letter" is it? What are its chief features, and how is it organized? Why do questions arise about its author? These issues will orient us to the document as a whole.

A Letter, Or—?

"The Epistle of Paul the Apostle to the Hebrews"—so runs the title found in the King James Version of the Bible. When we study the old manuscripts of the Greek New Testament, however, we find that the superscription did not appear until several centuries later. The earliest copies of Hebrews simply read, "To the Hebrews."

Indeed, on examination, Hebrews turns out to be a strange sort of letter. Think of letters we write and receive. They always start off with an addressee—"Dear Mary, . . ." "Gentlemen, . . ." Often the opening words contain a greeting or a short introductory statement. The body deals with the matter or matters of concern—expressions of love, items of business, information

13

requested or given, and so on. The remarks always contain a *personal* element. The writer, depending on the addressee and the purpose of writing, shares himself to a greater or lesser degree. The close likewise is formal: "Yours sincerely, Tom," or its equivalent.

The New Testament letters follow a similar pattern. See how Paul writes to the Christians in Galatia, Rome, Philippi, Colossae, Corinth, or to his friend Philemon. We find words of greeting, personal wishes, discussion of items as they come to mind, a stylized closing marked by mention of individuals, and a final Christian benediction. They resemble letters a Christian pastor today might write to a congregation he previously shepherded, or to a church member. The only significant difference is the beginning. Whereas we commence with the person(s) addressed ("Dear John . . .") and close with the writer's name ("Yours truly, Agnes"), Paul immediately identifies himself: "Paul, an apostle of Jesus Christ, . . . to the church at . . ."[1]

Now look at Hebrews. We find no identification of the author, no mention of the recipients, no word of greeting. Instead, the document plunges headlong into a profound theological statement: "In many and various ways God spoke . . ."[2] Nor does the writing show that spontaneous, itemized character, taking up topics, problems, or questions in turn, that we expect in a letter, but it follows the form of a measured argument that rolls on in calculated, steady flow—not, we might say, the mountain stream, with rapids, crosscurrents, side eddies, even whirlpools, of the letter form, but the broad reaches of a river cutting its inexorable track to the sea.

Hebrews is not a letter. The apostle himself calls it a "word of exhortation,"[3] and that should give us a hint. For neither is it a theological treatise, despite a common misunderstanding. Throughout the book, theology intertwines with practical concerns. How then shall we describe Hebrews? Best, as a sermon. Unlike a letter, which may arise out of deep emotion and be written at feverish pace (as was Galatians, for instance), a sermon results from careful planning. Yet it is not written in isolation from life—it continually has in mind hearers and their needs. So in the sermon to the Hebrews the theological reasoning, for all its (to us) complexity, serves a specific, practical end in the lives of its original recipients.

Already we are off and running in our search to understand Hebrews. The discussion about the nature of our document has made it more meaningful to us. Immediately we realize that to concentrate exclusively on the theological sections of the sermon will cause us to miss its basic purpose. And we are more ready to accept the possibility that this early sermon, meant to give spiritual help to early believers in Jesus Christ, may have something of importance for our everyday living also.

Let us try to find out more about "the Hebrews." Who were they, and what were their spiritual needs?

The Hebrews

The term "Hebrews" does not occur in the sermon. It occurs only in the title. While the earliest copies that we have agree on the title "To the Hebrews," they themselves are at least two hundred years removed from the autograph copy.

If the title is genuine, it has four possible interpretations. The first two are the most obvious. "Hebrews," used ethnically, refers either to the Jews in general (an apology for Christianity to the Jewish people) or to Jewish Christians. A third way of understanding "Hebrews" would be in a spiritual sense, i.e., to spiritual Jews, understanding the new Israel as the Christian church (1 Peter speaks throughout of Gentile Christians in such terms).[4] C. Spicq[5] has suggested a fourth—a metaphorical—sense of "Hebrews." On the analogy of Deuteronomy 26:5, where the original Hebrews were wanderers, he holds that the title of our sermon signifies "To the Wanderers." His idea finds support in the references to journeying found especially in chapters 3, 4, 11, and 13.[6]

On the basis of clear-cut data within Hebrews itself we may quickly set aside the first suggestion. Although some students of the Book of Hebrews have argued that the readers were either non- or part-Christian Jews, we may be sure they were

15

"complete" Christians. The book calls Jesus "Lord" (2:3). Its readers had received His salvation mediated through the apostles (2:1-4) and had been blessed with the gift of the Holy Spirit (6:4, 5). Indeed, they had been Christians for a considerable period of time, because their service on behalf of the saints was well known (6:9, 10), and formerly—at the time they became Christians—they had suffered hardship and loss because of their confession of Jesus (10:32-34).

Likewise the third interpretation fails. We do not find the apostle taking the Old Testament promises to Israel and applying them in a spiritual sense to Gentile believers as 1 Peter so obviously does. The book contains many references to the Old Testament, but uses them in one of two ways—either without "spiritualizing," as in the descriptions of the sacrificial system, or Messianically.[7]

Spicq's explanation of Hebrews as "wanderers" is ingenious. Unfortunately for the theory, however, we find no clear reference to Deuteronomy 26:5 within the text. It must therefore remain a conjecture. Perhaps Spicq was on the track of more than he realized, as we shall see when our understanding of Hebrews has run its full course (see chapter 8).

We have left the second possibility of Jewish Christians. For many students of Hebrews this answer was already obvious. They concluded that the extensive references to the Old Testament priesthood and cultus presuppose a Jewish-Christian audience, one perhaps that feels the pull of the old Temple services or which faces the trauma of the loss of the Temple in the Roman destruction of Jerusalem in AD 70.[8]

The case is not watertight, however. The appeal to the sacrificial argumentation must face three curious bits of evidence in the text. On one hand, the apostle does not reason from the services of the Temple supposedly current in his day. Rather, he argues from the sacrificial system of the wilderness Tabernacle.[9] That is, he does not work from contemporary Judaism but from the Pentateuch of the Old Testament. On the other hand, he is not careful in his description of the Old Testament Sanctuary and sacrifices. For instance, he locates the golden altar in the Most

Holy and merges the various sacrifices.[10] We wonder if such "lapses" would not have concerned a Jewish-Christian audience (we shall take up this matter again in chapter 5). The several appeals to the "living God" (3:12; 9:14; 10:31; 12:22) would have more significance if directed toward Gentile Christians.

We should add that much of the sacrificial argumentation would have added significance if the Jerusalem Temple were still erect and operating. On balance, then, the point of view that sees the readers as Jewish Christians has the stronger position, even if we do find some room for doubt.

One verse—and only one—appears to shed some light on the location of the readers. In 13:24 we read, "Those who come *from Italy* send you greetings." But even this is ambiguous. It can mean either (a) those domiciled in Italy, in which case Hebrews was composed from Italy (many scholars think from Rome);[11] or (b) those of Italian origin, in which case the author of Hebrews wrote to Christians in Italy (again, perhaps to Rome). Possibly we should prefer the latter on the basis of the Greek construction.

The question of the identity of the Hebrews is interesting, but it is not the main issue. Fortunately, we do not have to know for sure whether they were Jewish or Gentile Christians before we can understand the sermon written out for them. More important is their spiritual profile, which readily emerges as we look at the instruction they received.

We noticed above that the Hebrews were Christians of long standing. But therein lies a danger—our religion can become tired, the vital force can gradually ebb away. That was the problem facing the early believers addressed in the apostle's sermon.

In 2:1-4 the apostle's counsel focuses in the words *drift* or *slip* of verse 1 and *neglect* of verse 3. The first term is an interesting one in the Greek. It is a nautical metaphor used for flowing by, slipping away, being washed away, drifting away. As night winds and currents may carry a ship, apparently safe at anchor, out of the harbor, as it may lose its course, so Christians have to beware lest they drift from the harbor of salvation. The word can apply also to a ring that slips off the finger and is lost (hence the KJV "slip"). The idea is similar—the possibility of a gradual loss occurring unbeknown.

The second term, translated "neglect," signifies "disregard," "lack of concern." We note that it is *"so great salvation"* (KJV) or, as the NEB* has it, *"deliverance so great,"* that is at stake. The apostle is not here warning against a deliberate rejection of Christianity. Instead, he worries about the possibility of its neglect. It is because Christianity is so *precious* that we must not take it for granted. The value of the religion calls for a zeal that acknowledges its worth. When salvation is so great, how can the one who treats it casually escape divine retribution?

We find a second series of exhortations at 3:1-4:11. Here the word *harden* surfaces. The idea is similar to what we found at 2:1-4, although the metaphor has changed—that of the gradual loss of spiritual powers. It is the "heart" that hardens by the relentless inroads of the *apate* (deceitfulness, or pleasures) of sin. Such a heart—an evil, unfaithful heart—may lead at length to a falling away (literally, "apostasy"), a dropping out from the community, just as the children of Israel wandered away from devotion to the Lord and perished in the desert (3:7-15).

The apostle's counsel now takes on a new dimension. While he speaks of the hardening—the slow, insidious corrupting of the heart—he adds the ideas of disobedience and rebellion (3:16-19; 4:6, 11). Here we see a decline of religious experience that goes beyond mere neglect. In fact, the author raises the grim possibility that the subtle power of sin may even pervert the heart until it overtly defies its Lord.

A third section of the sermon, 5:11-6:20, sheds much light on the nature of the community and its spiritual dangers. The apostle now rebukes his hearers because of their lack of growth. They ought to be teachers, but instead need to learn the ABCs of God's oracles. Rather than developing to maturity, they are spiritual infants. They have become "dull of hearing" (5:11-14).

*From The New English Bible. Copyright, The Delegates of the Oxford University Press and The Syndics of the Cambridge University Press, 1961, 1970. Reprinted by permission.

The illustration from agriculture (6:7-12) drives the thought home. Land that receives bountiful rain must produce its harvest; otherwise it is accursed. Likewise, Christians should bear evidence of the blessings of God in their lives or they will lose them. The problem addressed resembles the one we have seen in the earlier exhortations against neglect and hardening of the heart. Here the author admonishes the readers, lest they become lazy or sluggish instead of maintaining a persevering faith to the end (6:11, 12).

At the same time we see a vivid picture of the possibility of open rejection of the values of the community. The warning at 6:4-6 is one of the most startling of the entire Bible and has evoked intense study by Christians from the earliest times. We shall deal with it at length later (see chapter 7). For now we need simply note the three key words in the portrayal of denial of Jesus: falling away (literally, *apostasy*, as in 3:12), "crucifying the Son of God" again (NEB) (or, crucifying "on their own account" [RSV], or with their own hands), and exposing Him to contempt (or "making mock of his death" [NEB]). It is a sad, grim picture. Could it be possible that someone blessed of the Spirit and nurtured on the Word of God could one day come to the point of open, public repudiation of Christ and His cross? Yes, says the apostle. Yes, even this. So be careful!

A fourth passage, 10:19-39, embodies the twofold dangers of neglect and rejection that we have noticed already. We find here, on the one hand, the peril of wavering, of neglecting the public assembly of the people of God, of forgetting the "former days" of Christian steadfastness, of casting away confidence in the certainty of the triumph of God's program, and of shrinking back (verses 23-25, 32-39). But we find also a passage strikingly reminiscent of 6:4-6. Here the Christian sins willfully (deliberately, with a high hand), spurning the Son of God, profaning the blood of the covenant, and outraging the Spirit (verses 26-31).

The apostle returns to exhortation in the final two chapters of his sermon. His advice shows that his hearers face the danger of growing weary, that under the hardships of Christian life they may gradually drop out. They may neglect to show hospitality or to remember their fellows, or they may fall into idolatry, immorality, the love of money, or the snare of false teachings (12:3-14; 13:1-9). At the same time he introduces the example of Esau (12:15-17). He was *bebēlos,* that is, profane, godless, irreligious. Due to his disregard for spiritual privileges he eventually lost the blessing of the birthright and found no way to recover it. In the same way the peril of rejection and refusal always remains a fearsome possibility for the Christians. "See that you do not refuse him who is speaking" (12:25).

These passages have given us a fairly clear spiritual profile of the recipients of Hebrews. Their problem is not false teachers who have swept their young feet off the ground, as in Galatia. Nor is it a heady enthusiasm because of manifestations of the Spirit, as in Corinth. It is not the question of the failure of the Jews to receive the gospel, as in Romans. No, their problem is one of *tired blood.* They have grown weary with waiting for the Lord's return, sluggish in their Christian identity, questioning the value of their religion, more so as hard times for Christians appear to loom on the horizon.

Spiritual weariness is dangerous is the apostle's message. Over and over, as we have seen, he hammers home its fearful results. Either, he suggests, we grow neglectful of our privileges, taking lightly what is of supreme value, or we may turn in defiant rejection of the entire Christian faith, taking our place among the majority who do not confess Jesus as Saviour and Lord. One end is as dire as the other.

But it is one thing to diagnose the malady. To provide healing often proves much more difficult. Let us see how the apostle goes about prescribing a remedy.

Features of the Apostle's Sermon

A passage with apparently curious logic provides a clue to his line of attack. We referred above to 5:11-14, where he upbraided the Hebrews for their lack of spiritual growth. Let us take another look at it.

20

The apostle, in 5:1-10, has embarked upon a careful consideration of the high priesthood of Jesus, bouncing the discussion off the Aaronic priests. He arrives at the point of Jesus' Melchizedekian priesthood—and abruptly stops. In fact, he doesn't get back to Melchizedek until the end of the next chapter. "About Melchizedek we have much to say," he writes, "much that is difficult to explain, now that you have grown so dull of hearing" (verse 11, NEB). Then follows the rebuke that they are still infants instead of mature Christians.

But notice how he proceeds. In view of his statement at verse 12 that they need "milk" instead of solid food, we would expect him to bring out the baby's bottle. Apparently they won't be able to digest the heavy doctrine about Melchizedek. So, at 6:1 we *expect* him to say, "Let us then go back to the elementary ideas of Christianity. Since you aren't ready for solid food, we'll have to leave Melchizedek alone!" But instead he says just the opposite: *"Let us then stop discussing the rudiments of Christianity"* (6:1, NEB). What sort of strange reasoning is this?

It is the conjunction "then" or "therefore" (Greek, *dio*) that makes his logic so curious. We must not dilute its force. In essence, the apostle reasons: "You aren't ready for solid food, but only for milk; *therefore* let us leave aside milk and give you solid food."

And, of course, that is just what he does. After the exhortations of chapter 6 he launches into the most convoluted logic of the whole sermon as he argues about Melchizedek, Abraham, and Jesus. Chapter 7 of Hebrews is one of the most difficult chapters to understand in the entire Bible. Likewise, 8:1-10:18, while not quite so involved, develops the priestly ministry and sacrifice of Jesus in a highly complex argumentation.

How shall we account for the *therefore* at 6:1? Exegetes of Hebrews have almost stood on their heads as they have tried to get around it. Some have suggested, for instance, two groups among the Hebrews—one spiritually retarded and the other developed. The apostle rebukes the first at 5:11-14 and then goes on to give the advanced teaching about Melchizedek and Christ's ministry to those able to appreciate it. The problem with this interpretation is that it entirely lacks support in the text. As we saw in the previous section, the author directs his counsels toward *all* his hearers—we have no hint of a differentiation such as the one suggested.

When we meditate long enough on 5:11-6:1, its logic at last strikes home. The apostle, aware of the spiritual problems of his hearers, has thought through carefully to a solution. They have failed to grow and still are ready only for milk—*but milk will not help them any longer.* Their situation is serious. If they are to be saved from the perils of neglect or rejection, they must take solid food. The *therefore* suggests that *their only hope* is in what he is about to lay before them.

His emphasis upon intellectual activity is unique among the writings of the New Testament. The apostle declares that theology—even difficult theology—aids Christian growth. In at least some cases of stagnation, the *only hope* will come through the solid food of theology.[12]

Now we begin to grasp why the sermon to the Hebrews is as it is. It has long been a source of inquiry as Christians have wrestled with its theological complexities. Yet, as we have already learned, the apostle directed it toward a highly practical end, as every sermon should be. That is, the pamphlet blends theology and exhortation, each part dovetailing into the other. In other words, the apostle advances theology in the service of the exhortation, it being the "solid food" that the apostle thinks indispensable to improve the spiritual condition of the Hebrews. Likewise, the exhortations arise out of the theology. It is *in view of* the theology presented that Christians are not to neglect "such a great salvation."

This insight into the place of theology in Hebrews enables us to grasp another of its special features. If we look closely at the document, we begin to notice an *alternation* of theology and exhortation. We readily recognize the latter by the change from the third person to the first or second person plural, usually with the hortatory "let us . . ." and often with the conjunction "therefore." For instance, all the first chapter involves theological discourse, but as soon as we come to chapter 2, we notice,

"Therefore we must pay the closer attention . . ."

The first four verses are no longer theological but instead divert from theology (or better, *apply* the theology) in exhortation. At 2:5, the apostle reverts to the third person and has clearly moved back on the theological track.

Thus, the following laminated pattern of Hebrews emerges:

Theology	1:1-14
Exhortation	2:1-4
Theology	2:5–3:6a
Exhortation	3:6b–4:16
Theology	5:1-10
Exhortation	5:11–6:20
Theology	7:11–0:18
Exhortation	10:19–13:25

The discerning reader will have observed that we have already employed this pattern. In our search for the spiritual profile of the Hebrews we had, in fact, raked through the exhortations of the sermon.

We may mention three more features of the sermon to the Hebrew Christians. They are all of a theological nature and are worth noting here as we seek to gain an overview of the document. With our understanding of the high place given to theology in Hebrews, we can now better appreciate their significance.

First, Hebrews is unique among the New Testament writings for its presentation of the high-priestly Christology. Elsewhere we find, at the most, hints, such as in Romans 8:34 or 1 John 2:2, or allusive imagery as in Revelation, chapters 1, 4, and 5. In Hebrews, however, Jesus as High Priest is a dominant idea, and the book works it out in great detail.

Second, the writing contains much "cultic" terminology—that is, references to temples, sacrifices, priests, blood, and ablutions. The use of such language extends beyond the high-priestly Christology and the theological sections. It occurs as early as 1:3, which mentions that Jesus makes "purification for sins." Often we fail to catch its force in the English. But consider the following verses, almost all of which are of a hortatory nature (only 10:1

comes in a strictly theological section):

4:16: "Let us then with confidence *draw near* to the throne of grace."

7:25: "Consequently he is able . . . to save those who *draw near* to God through him."

10:1: "Sacrifices which are continually offered . . . make perfect those who *draw near*."

10:22: "Let us *draw near* with a true heart in full assurance of faith."

11:6: "For whoever would *draw near* to God must believe that he exists."

12:18-22: "For you have not *come* to what may be touched. . . . You have *come* to Mount Zion."

In each case the italicized words are forms of the verb *proserchomai*, used for the approach of the priest into the Divine Presence in the Temple. That is, the apostle speaks of the "drawing near" of the people of God in terms of a system of Temple and sacrifice.[13]

Third, Hebrews is unique in its *systematic* presentation of theological argument. The apostle thought out the whole work before he wrote the first word. He introduces each idea in its correct place, then develops and rounds it off. Each motif blends into the total argument to produce a composition of great logical force. Apart from its spiritual powers, the document is a masterpiece of ordered thinking.[14] (And so we ought to note every word with great care—more so than in some more hurried works, where we look for the *ideas*.) For instance, notice the following ideas of Hebrews:

a. Purification: introduced at 1:3, developed in 9:1–10:18.

b. High priest: introduced at 2:17, 18, expanded at 4:14-16 and 5:1-10, fully expounded at 7:1–10:18.

c. Angels: introduced at 1:4, developed in 1:5-14, wound up at 2:16.

d. Covenant: introduced at 7:22, developed in 8:6-13, rounded off at 9:18 and 10:16-18.

e. Faith: introduced at 2:17, expanded in 3:1-6, full development in 11:1-39.

The Key Message of the Sermon

Out of the interplay of theology and exhortation, out of the finely woven structure, what "message" emerges? With all the involved theological aspects of the sermon and with his concerns about the spiritual ailments of his hearers and their future, can we put our finger on *one* central idea?

I suggest that 10:19-23 sums up the sermon better than any other passage. "Therefore, brethren, since we have confidence to enter the sanctuary by the blood of Jesus, by the new and living way which he opened for us through the curtain, that is, through his flesh, and since we have a great priest over the house of God, let us draw near with a true heart in full assurance of faith, with our hearts sprinkled clean from an evil conscience and our bodies washed with pure water. Let us hold fast the confession of our hope without wavering, for he who promised is faithful."

We will come back to these words throughout our book. Let us briefly notice the great ideas here, however.

First of all, a "therefore" introduces the passage. Indeed, as we look back over our structure of Hebrews, we notice that it comes at the conclusion of the longest theological section of the pamphlet, 7:1–10:18. As we shall see later, the argument of Hebrews reaches a glorious climax here, closing the theology proper in the sermon. The long exhortation that commences at 10:19 runs to the end of the work.

So we see 10:19-21 summing up the great truths that the apostle has developed from 1:1 on and which have come to full fruit in 7:1–10:18. He tells us that *the way* to the heavenly sanctuary *is open,* that we have full access through the "flesh" of Jesus. Not only did He break the path for us, but He Himself is *our heavenly High Priest.* It is these superlatives that embody "such a great salvation" first spoken of at 2:3.

And *because—therefore! Therefore* let us "draw near" in full assurance. *Therefore* let us be firm and unswerving in our confession of hope. In other words, the *what* of the Christian religion calls for a corresponding *so what* from those who know it.

Here we have a sermon for weary Christians, a message to stir up Christian growth and zeal. Instead of sluggishness, spiritual inertia, shrinking back in view of the long delay in the return of the Lord, they are to be fully assured. Fully assured of what Christ *has done,* of *where* and *what* He is, of what He *will do.* And fully assured of their own cleansing from sin.

The New American Bible* translates 10:22: "Let us draw near in utter sincerity and absolute confidence, our hearts sprinkled clean from the evil which lay on our conscience and our bodies washed in pure water."

"In absolute confidence"—this expression summarizes the message of Hebrews as we understand it. It will be our goal in the remaining chapters of this book to fully unlock it. We must see its *bases*—why may Christians now live "in absolute confidence"? The answers are theological, five in number, and we shall devote a chapter to each. And then, having worked through the theological bases of absolute confidence, we shall examine its *nature.* That will involve us in a deeper look at the exhortations of Hebrews as we study in turn the severe warnings of the writing and the call for "faith." For a final chapter we shall look once again to Hebrews *as a whole,* seeking for our last impression to gain a total grasp of the enigmatic document in the light of all our studies in "absolute confidence."

We are now ready for an outline of Hebrews:
A. The proem (1:1-4)
B. Christ superior to the angels (1:5-14)
C. The first exhortation (2:1-4)
D. Christ's temporary inferiority to angels—the necessity of the incarnation (2:5-18)
E. Christ superior to Moses (3:1-6a)
F. The second exhortation—"Rest" (3:6b–4:16)
   1. Lessons from Israel (3:6b-19)
   2. Application to Christians (4:1-16)
G. Characteristics of high priests (5:1-10)

H. The third exhortation (5:11-6:20)
  1. Rebuke (5:11-14)
  2. Warning (6:1-6)
  3. Encouragement (6:7-20)
I. Jesus Christ, High Priest and Sacrifice (7:1-10:18)
  1. A better order of priesthood (chapter 7)
  2. A better sanctuary (8:1-6)
  3. A better covenant (8:7-13)
  4. A better sacrifice (9:1-10:18)—"better blood"
    a. Brief description of the earthly sanctuary (9:1-5)
    b. Limitations of the old cultus (9:6-10)
    c. Summary of the new cultus (9:11-14)
    d. "Objective" benefits of the new cultus (9:15-28)
    e. "Subjective" benefits of the new cultus (10:1-18)
J. The final exhortation (10:19-13:25)
  1. Response in view of Christ's work (10:19-39)
  2. Examples of faith (11:1-39)
  3. Encouragement and warning (12:1-29)
    a. The example of Jesus (12:1-11)
    b. Encouragement (12:12-14)
    c. Warning (12:15-17)
    d. Blessings (12:18-24)
    e. Warnings (12:25-29)
  4. Concluding exhortations (13:1-25)

The Apostle

Some Christians manifest an undue concern over the identity of the author of Hebrews. It is almost as though it were more important to find out who he is than to wrestle with understanding his ideas.

The question of authorship is intriguing, of course. Who, we wonder, could have put together such a masterly work? Was it possible that someone unknown to us out of the early church could have been its author?

He (or she?[15]) did not identify himself, and thereby gave rise to a history of speculation. We know that in the century after

27

its composition the authorship of Hebrews provided a topic of Christian conversation. Clement of Alexandria in the 190s discussed the matter and concluded that Paul wrote Hebrews in the Hebrew language, while Luke translated it into Greek. A few years later, however, Origen, also of Alexandria and the finest scholar of his time, was unsure:

"If I gave my opinion, I should say that the thoughts are those of the apostle, but the diction and phraseology are those of some one who remembered the apostolic teachings, and wrote down at his leisure what had been said by his teacher. Therefore if any church holds that this epistle is by Paul, let it be commended for this. For not without reason have the ancients handed it down as Paul's. But who wrote the epistle, in truth, God knows. The statement of some who have gone before us is that Clement, bishop of the Romans, wrote the epistle, and of others that Luke, the author of the Gospel and the Acts, wrote it. But let this suffice on these matters." [16]

The question of authorship delayed the universal acceptance of Hebrews into the New Testament canon. A test of canonicity was apostolicity. Each writing had to be from the hand of an apostle or one associated with an apostle. But what of Hebrews? The Western churches considered Paul its author, while the Eastern churches remained in doubt for several centuries. Eventually, however, the Pauline view prevailed, and the church generally accepted the writing.

Many Christians assert that surely Paul, the theologian of the early church, must have written Hebrews. But the position has problems both of language and ideas. The actual Greek of Hebrews is utterly unlike that of the Pauline letters in terms of both syntax and vocabulary. But if we allow a large enough measure of freedom to a Pauline scribe (and Paul did employ scribes; see, for example, Romans 16:22 and Galatians 6:11), the difficulty might be surmountable. The ideas of Hebrews, however, are different from those in Paul's other writings. Apart from the high-priestly argumentation, found only here, the book discusses the ways in which "law" and "faith" are used (see chapters 4 and 6). Further, the writer does not speak of himself as an apostle (see 2:3, 4; 13:6, 7)—something quite the opposite of Paul's language in his letters (see, for example, Romans 1:1, 5; 1 Corinthians 1:1; 2 Corinthians 1:1; Galatians 1:1–2:10).

Sensitive to such distinctions, few scholars, whether "liberal" or "conservative," hold to a Pauline authorship for Hebrews. Over the centuries they have suggested a variety of people, ranging from Peter and Apollos (Luther) even to a woman, Prisca (von Harnack)! But the question remains unresolved. We simply do not have a total enough view of the early Christian church to settle the issue if we do not take Paul as the author.

The question of authorship of Hebrews cuts with particular power among Seventh-day Adventists. Ellen G. White, in many incidental references,[17] attributes the document to Paul. On occasion, however, she simply refers to "the apostle."[18] So the matter ultimately probes far deeper than the immediate issue of identity. It has implications for the manner and meaning of the inspiration of Ellen G. White.

It will now be obvious that, whatever view one holds, some difficulties will remain. Those who contend for the Pauline authorship must admit a degree of freedom allowed his scribe that other students would find unacceptable. To attempt to identify any other writer will rest almost entirely on speculation.

In view of such problems, I prefer simply to adopt the Ellen G. White designation of "the apostle." It has the advantage of eliminating at a stroke those fears with regard to canonicity which some may feel when we do not specifically designate Paul. Further, such a position does not categorically *deny* Pauline origin. Many scholars of the New Testament have stated that, whoever wrote Hebrews, it was certainly *not* Paul. Given our extremely scanty knowledge of the actual New Testament churches and the twenty-seven documents in our canon, I would not go so far. That the document may be in some sense Pauline is altogether a possibility. We cannot forget its placement among the Pauline writings in some old manuscripts of the New Testament.

Finally, however, I consider the quest for identification a futile one. It involves too many imponderables. Far better,

29

then, to call our author "the apostle" and get on with
the job of understanding his message.

Hebrews and Christian Life Today

Our study of Hebrews has already shown how valuable this
ancient sermon may be to Christians approaching the close of the
second millennium after Christ. Our *condition,* our *need,* our
preaching—it illumines all of them.

The portrait of the recipients of Hebrews seems strikingly
modern. If the passage of the years troubled those early
Christians—the seemingly relentless flow of time, uninterrupted
by divine event—how much more so today. It is a sad fact that a
great many Christians abandoned the hope of the Second Coming
long ago. Modern theories—the evolution of the race, the uniform
processes of change, decay, and new life, the inevitability of
progress—have shaped twentieth-century thought. Indeed, in our
age the scientist has become high priest, and the nostrums of the
psychologist and sociologist provide balm for (apparently) every
malady. When man has been, as it were, analyzed, dissected, and
probed, when he seems to fit in with and conform to the natural
order, what room remains for a specifically *religious* dimension?

Then we have the continual pressure of a secular way of
thought and life. Christendom, if ever it existed, collapsed with
the onset of World War I. We have entered a new Dark Ages for
the Christian Church, with enormous threats to a truly Christian
way in the world. Its temptations are subtle, its allurements
beguiling. The high drop-out rate among Christians, especially
teenagers, should not surprise us, even if it does distress us.

Drop out—or slowly dry up. That is the second danger, as real
today as when the apostle penned his sermon. Worship becomes
a form, prayer a lifeless ritual, church membership a ticket in the
Christian "club." One may choose to come and go, to leave and
rejoin, almost willy-nilly.

Our *need,* then, is to hear the same sort of message as the
Hebrews. Someone must remind us of the *reality* of our religion,
of its surpassing *worth*—must tell us again of the glory of our

Head. And tell us in such a way that we can grasp it, that it brings us to our senses. Once more we must hear that because our religion is so great, we must take it *seriously*. Perhaps if we can grasp the magnificence of our salvation, if we can see the transcendent dimension, the divine realities of it, then we will cease to be so wishy-washy as Christians. Then we may stand up on our feet and look the world squarely in the eye. Then we shall know for sure *who* we are and *what* we are to be.

Absolute confidence—surely here is our need. In the face of the man-centered confidence of the secular age, in defiance of its nonchalant passing by of God and His Word, we need absolute confidence in Him and His rule. We need absolute confidence of our own standing before Him, in the certainty of the triumph of His kingdom.

But suddenly the world is not so sure of itself. Human progress no longer seems inevitable. The close of the second millennium comes with dark prophecies of gloom from the scientists and futurologists as they see the world running out of fossil-fuel energy, clean air, fresh water, food. A secular apocalyptic fills the air. That world also needs to hear the message of absolute confidence borne by Hebrews.

Preachers who have read this chapter will have learned much. The apostle tells us, first of all, that *theology* is important in preaching. To work and talk revival is meaningless unless it has its necessary theological accompaniment. Likewise, merely to tell the people what they ought to be and do is not enough—to harangue with exhortation is a failure. Perhaps preachers have served up milk for too long. Maybe they themselves need first to dig deeply into the mine of the Word and bring forth, like Matthew's scribe, treasures old and new. Only as the people receive solid food can we expect changes.

Likewise, we must preach to a *need*. We must carefully think through the spiritual problems of the people and pray and study until we know how to meet them with a blend of theology and exhortation. Too many "sermons" are lectures, interesting discourses. Few arise out of a burning conviction and desire to address human need.

31

It is time for us to begin our study of the five bases of absolute confidence in Hebrews. They are all theological, as we would expect. We turn now to the first as we consider "One who is Son."

---

[1] Romans 1:1, 7; 1 Corinthians 1:1-3; 2 Corinthians 1:1, 2; Galatians 1:1-5; Ephesians 1:1, 2; Philippians 1:1, 2; Colossians 1:1, 2; 1 Thessalonians 1:1; 2 Thessalonians 1:1, 2; 1 Timothy 1:1, 2; 2 Timothy 1:1, 2; Titus 1:1-4; Philemon 1-3; cf. James 1:1; 1 Peter 1:1; 2 Peter 1:1; Jude 1. Notice the personalized closing also, e.g. Romans 16:1-27; 1 Corinthians 16:5-24; Galatians 6:11-18; Philippians 4:14-23; Colossians 4:7-18; 2 Timothy 4:9-22; Titus 3:12-15; Philemon 23-25.

[2] All Biblical references are to the Revised Standard Version unless otherwise acknowledged.

[3] Hebrews 13:22.

[4] 1 Peter 1:1; 2:4-9; 3:5, 6, 18-22.

[5] C. Spicq, *L'Epître aux Hébreux* (2 vols., Paris: Gabalda, 1952). Vol. 1, pp. 269-80; esp. 243-46; also "L'Epître aux Hébreux: Apollos, Jean-Baptiste, les Hellénistes et Qumrân," *RevQ*, Vol. 1 (1958-1959), pp. 365-90.

[6] Hebrews 3:7–4:11; 11:8-10, 13-16, 27, 37, 38; 13:11-14. See later under chapter 8—"Christianity as Pilgrimage."

[7] In chapter 5, "The Sacrifice—Once for All," we shall take up the Old Testament references for close study. For examples of a Messianic understanding of the Old Testament, see Hebrews 1:5-13; 2:6-8, 12, 13; 5:5, 6; 7:1-3, 11, 17, 21.

[8] This is the view set out in M. L. Andreasen's *The Book of Hebrews* (Washington, D.C.: Review and Herald, 1948), pp. 21-31, 34-42.

[9] See Hebrews 8:5; 9:1-8.

[10] Hebrews 9:3, 4. Despite many efforts scholars have advanced no convincing explanation. Note the merging of "goats and bulls" (Hebrews 9:13), "calves and goats" (9:19), and "bulls and goats" (10:4). Compare the Old Testament text to which 9:15-22 alludes. Instead of "calves and goats" it mentions only "oxen" (Exodus 24:3-8).

[11] William Manson, in *The Epistle to the Hebrews: An Historical and Theological Reconsideration.* (Edinburgh: Hodder & Stoughton, 1951) most persuaively presented the case for Rome.

[12] "The agency of the Spirit of God does not remove from us the necessity of exercising our faculties and talents, but teaches us how to use every power to the glory of God. The human faculties, when under the special direction of the grace of God, are capable of being used to the best purpose on earth. Ignorance does not increase the humility or spirituality of any professed follower of Christ. The truths of the divine word can be best appreciated by an intellectual Christian. Christ can be best glorified by those who serve Him intelligently"

(Ellen G. White, *Counsels to Parents, Teachers, and Students*, p. 361).

[13] I have explored the cultic terminology of Hebrews in my PhD dissertation, *Defilement and Purgation in the Book of Hebrews* (Vanderbilt University, 1973).

[14] Edmund Gosse, in a magnificent passage from *Father and Son*, has captured the force of the language and ideas of Hebrews. " 'The extraordinary beauty of the language—for instance, the matchless cadences and images of the first chapter—made a certain impression upon my imagination, and were (I think) my earliest initiation into the magic of literature. I was incapable of defining what I felt, but I certainly had a grip in the throat, which was in its essence a purely aesthetic emotion, when my father read, in his pure, large, ringing voice, such passages as "The heavens are the work of Thy hands. They shall perish, but Thou remainest, and they shall all wax old as doth a garment, and as a vesture shalt Thou fold them up, and they shall be changed; but Thou art the same, and Thy years shall not fail." But the dialectic parts of the epistle puzzled and confused me. Such metaphysical ideas as "laying again the foundation of repentance from dead works" and "crucifying the Son of God afresh" were not successfully brought down to the level of my understanding. . . . The melodious language, the divine forensic audacities, the magnificent ebb and flow of argument which make the Epistle to the Hebrews such a miracle, were far beyond my reach, and they only bewildered me' " (quoted in James Moffatt, *A Critical and Exegetical Commentary on the Epistle to the Hebrews* [Edinburgh: T. & T. Clark, 1924]).

[15] Among the many suggestions for the author of Hebrews, one is a woman—Prisca (Priscilla), wife of Aquila and friend of Paul.

[16] Quoted by Eusebius, *Ecclesiastical History*, vi. 25.

[17] *The Great Controversy*, pp. 347, 411-13, 415, 420, 512; *Patriarchs and Prophets*, p. 357; *Sons and Daughters of God*, p. 24; *Testimonies*, Vol. 1, p. 679; Vol. 5, p. 651; Vol. 8, pp. 79, 80; *Testimony Treasures*, Vol. 2, p. 267.

[18] *Testimonies*, Vol. 4, p. 618; Vol. 6, p. 342; Vol. 8, p. 115; *Adventist Home*, p. 445; *Testimony Treasures*, Vol. 2, p. 569.

Chapter 2

The Son— God's Climactic Speech

Poor old Sisyphus! The king from Greek mythology was consigned to endless frustration. The gods sentenced him to push a huge stone up an incline in Hades—only to have it roll back, over and over again, just as he got it to the top.

In the thinking of many twentieth-century people, *we* are Sisyphus. Life on Planet Earth seems a cosmic rat race, a weary round of birth, decay, and death. Cast up out of the primeval slime by some dimly perceived force, humanity in each cycle lives its little day but passes into nothingness. The dance of life, for all its color and movement, finds meaning only in its inevitable finale—the relapse into the primeval nothingness.

"Behold the . . . stars, how high they are!" exclaims the Book of Job.[1] But the telescope and technology of space have made us acutely aware of the vast reaches of emptiness. They have shown us how puny is earth, a speck in the universe, separated from everything else by mind-boggling, cold, dark distances.

What *are* we, we who inhabit earth? Are we alone amid the cosmic reaches? Are we victims of blind chance—or worse, of a cosmic sadist[2]—forever to grope in mystery as to our origin and being? How shall we break the shell of our finiteness, our isolation, and peer into the yolk of our existence?

But wait. What if, across the illimitable reaches of darkness and silence, a Voice should come? What if Someone—One not bound to our treadmill of birth-decay-death—should speak? Would it not transform all our living?

Hebrews asserts precisely that. The apostle's first words smash the riddle and dilemma of human existence: "In many and various ways God spoke." It is the *fact* of the speaking God that forms the first basis of absolute confidence for the Christian.

Notice that the apostle does not attempt to *prove* God's speaking here. Rather, he simply makes two great affirmations—there is a God and He reveals Himself. We cannot, after all, establish God by man's rational powers. He doesn't come as the third step of a syllogism, He can't be measured and weighed in the laboratory. No scientist, no mathematician, no philosopher, can come up with an argument and say, "Look! I've proved that there is a God." God is too big to be encompassed by man's mind in this way. (Likewise, we cannot disprove Him, despite what the atheist may attempt.[3])

And He is the speaking God. That is all important. Suppose God existed but forever chose to remain in His eternal remoteness. We would have no way of finding what He was like or even if He was. The mystery of our own being would remain. But God, because He speaks, communicates. That Voice shows us Himself and reveals ourselves.

In this chapter we shall look carefully to see how the apostle elaborates the idea of the speaking God. Clearly the matter is the first and prime basis for Christian confidence. If he was wrong at this point, all else will be useless. We shall observe that, while he does not set about to *prove* God, he refers to many evidences of God. Since God reveals Himself, we can see and hear indications of Him that we can examine and weigh.

The Speaking God

The name *God* occurs no less than sixty-seven times in Hebrews. The apostle prefers the term, occasionally using

"Lord"[4] and avoiding the term "Father," used frequently in the New Testament.[5]

Nor are the many references incidental in nature. No matter what turns the ongoing argument of Hebrews may take, behind all stands the figure of God. He is the Divine Shaper of history. Perhaps 3:4 sums up the idea best: "the founder of all is God"(NEB). Though it is the Son who commands attention in Hebrews, the apostle terms Him the "Son of God."[6] On the other hand, the book has only a few comparatively minor mentions to the Holy Spirit.[7]

Frequent references occur to the *will* of God. He wills the sufferings and death of the Son for us all (2:10), appoints Moses to service (3:2-5) and Aaron to high-priestly office, and designates Jesus as "high priest after the order of Melchizedek" (5:4-10). To do His will should be the constant concern of Christians (10:36).

Yet the apostle gives little space to actually describing God Himself. He merely refers to the *fact* of His existence (1:1-3) and mentions His glory (1:3; 9:5; 13:21) and His wrath: "Our God is a consuming fire" (12:29). Instead, the emphasis centers on the divine *activity*.[8]

So God made all things by His word (11:3) and gives promises to mankind, making the future doubly sure by adding an oath (6:17, 18). He brings blessing and curse (6:7, 8), provides grace (4:16), and acts fairly, remembering deeds of loving service done toward the saints (6:10). God brings peace (13:20), warns (12:25), and can deliver from death (5:7), even raising the dead to life (11:19).

And He is the God who enters into personal relations with mankind. The term "covenant," which we shall notice in subsequent chapters, describes His divine activity. "I will be their God, and they shall be my people" (Hebrews 8:10) is the goal of the covenant. The Source of all life condescends to engage in a human social structure to demonstrate His concern for mankind. So the apostle calls God's people a "household" (3:6, NEB), and through hard times the Christian may know that a divine Father permits for his good whatever happens (12:3-11).

We must never take Him for granted. Though He delights to

36

have man know Him personally, "it is a fearful thing to fall into the hands of the living God" (10:31). Concerned lest man abuse a covenant relationship, "He finds fault" with Israel (8:8). He is the Judge of all, and the man or woman who would spurn His grace and mock at His Son and His sacrifice must reckon with His wrath (10:26-31). The designation "living God," used four times,[9] carries with it the nuance of the personal, judgmental aspect of the divine activity. (So Hebrews, which perhaps has the greatest message of Christian confidence in the entire New Testament, also presents its severest warnings.)

Indubitably, however, the supreme divine activity is speaking. Forms of the verb "to speak" occur in connection with God fourteen times, and of "to say" another twenty-two times, a total of thirty-six usages in the sermon. His word comes with power and authority. It creates the universe (1:3), designates the superiority of the Son to angels (1:5-14), comes as warning (3:7-11), and guarantees fulfillment (4:1-10). So the admonition of the apostle is, "See that you do not refuse to hear the voice that speaks. Those who refused to hear the oracle speaking on earth found no escape; still less shall we escape if we refuse to hear the One who speaks from heaven" (12:25, 26, NEB).

Because of the apostle's emphasis on the speech of God, Scripture occupies an unusually high place in his sermon. Although he interlaces his work with quotations and allusions from the Old Testament (twenty-nine direct citations and another fifty-three possible allusions),[10] nowhere does he identify the Old Testament writer.[11] No matter who may have been the human author, every word of the Old Testament is ultimately the Word of God, even where we would not expect it. For example, when the author quotes the words of Isaiah 8:17, 18, which have primary reference to Isaiah and his sons—"Here am I, and the children God has given me"—he attributes the passage to the Son (2:12, 13). Again, whereas Genesis 2:2 describes the Sabbath resting of God in the third person, Hebrews takes the words and puts them into God's mouth (4:3-5).

The manner in which the apostle introduces the Old Testament quotations corresponds with his high view of Scripture.

Whereas in Romans, for instance, Paul begins the Old Testament passages with either "It stands written . . ." (sixteen times in Romans) or "Isaiah says . . ." (see, for example, Romans 10:16, 19, 20; 11:9), in Hebrews we find the following:

"He [God] says . . ." (e.g., 1:5-13; 5:5).

"He [Christ] says . . ." (e.g., 2:13; 10:5-9).

"The Holy Spirit says . . ." (3:7-9; 10:15).

"Somewhere it says . . ." (2:6).

What about God's speaking—is it merely in words? Clearly not. In 4:12, 13 we have a famous passage which declares that the word of God is alive and active, cutting and dividing, sifting the thoughts and purposes, laying bare the innermost soul. The construction here is interesting. The apostle begins by describing the "word of God," but by the close of the sentence has merged impersonal word with the personalized "him." It seems evident that the word of God, while not God, comes with a living quality and force because it *is God's*. We must never reduce it to syllables separated from the divine will, authority, and power.

The opening words of the sermon show the same idea. "God spoke . . . *by* the prophets. . . . He has spoken . . . *by* a Son" (1:1, 2). The preposition translated as "by" in both cases by the RSV is actually *en,* which we may understand as "in" as some commentators do. If so, the apostle is suggesting that the divine speaking is not merely by means of the words of the prophets or the Son. Rather, God spoke *in* them—their very being, their lives, experiences, and character manifested the word of God.

Truly, the God of Hebrews is a God who speaks. He spoke in ancient times, He spoke in the Son, He continues to speak through Scripture. We turn now to His climactic speech.

The Son

References to God frame the sermon to the Hebrews. He is the One who spoke of old and has spoken decisively in the Son (1:1, 2), and He is the One who raised the Son from the dead and gives grace to all (13:20, 25). In all the play and counterplay of human events He is *there*, behind the scenes or dimly perceived in the backdrop, working out His will.

On center stage, however, stands another. He plays the lead role in the drama of the ages. While it is God's will that He carries out, He Himself commands our chief attention. All eyes focus on Him. He is the Son.

We notice how the opening paragraph, the proem of 1:1-4, directs our gaze from the backdrop of God to the Son and turns the spotlight on Him.[12] The passage is a great piece of work. It is more than simply an introduction, but rather an anticipation and a summary of the entire theology of Hebrews.

The first division of thought in chapter 1 runs from verse 1 to 2a: "In many and various ways God spoke of old to our fathers by the prophets; but in these last days he has spoken to us by a Son." Here the apostle introduces us to the God who speaks, as we noticed above. He has carefully balanced the thought, as the following diagram shows:

The Old Revelation	*The New Revelation*
In many and various ways	
God spoke	God has spoken
to the forefathers	to us
of old	in the last of these days
in (by) the prophets	in the Son

Only one phrase has no direct match—the opening words, "In many and various ways." Putting it first also heightens the emphasis. What is the apostle trying to underline by his construction? Surely, the *fragmentary* character of the old revelation.

His words remind us of the Old Testament record of the divine speaking. It came in many different *episodes*—in the Garden; to Noah, who found grace in the eyes of the Lord; to Abram under the terebinths of Mamre; to Jacob, lying with a stone for his pillow at Bethel; to Moses at the burning bush; to Israel at Sinai (the high point of the Old Testament divine speech, as 12:18-21 brings out); to the boy Samuel in the Temple; to David as he followed the sheep; to Elijah the Tishbite and Elisha, his disciple; to that line of men and women called to be prophets and prophetesses. Truly, the God of the Old Testament is a speaking God.

And that speech came in various *modes*. Face-to-face, as in the Garden, by visions and dreams, by the thunders of Sinai, by the "still small voice" out of the cave in Beersheba, by the prophetic utterance, by Urim and Thummim—by all such means God revealed Himself anciently.

But—and here is the apostle's point—the *episodic* and *variegated* nature of the Old Testament speaking shows its incompleteness. The fact of its repetition indicates its partial, fragmentary character.

So he has prepared us for the contrast. Anciently God spoke, and spoke, and spoke again. But now He *has spoken*. He has uttered the decisive word. All that fragmentary Old Testament revelation was but an anticipation of the climactic "speech" of God. In the Son He has spoken with finality. All divine revelation before (and after—though Hebrews does not take up that possibility) must look to the Son for its hallmark.[13]

Thus the apostle does not leave the phrase "in many and various ways" dangling. It implies the corresponding term—"with finality." We may go back to our diagram now and complete it:

The God Who Speaks

Old Testament Speaking	New Testament Speaking
God spoke	God has spoken
to the forefathers	to us
of old	in the last of these days
in (by) the prophets	in the Son
incomplete (many and various ways)	with finality

Such considerations alert us to a *balance* between the old and the new. On the one hand, the apostle does not put down the Old Testament. Far from it. It is the record of the speaking of God. But on the other, he draws a contrast. The New Testament is not merely a continuation of the Old. While the one God stands

40

behind both, there is a qualitative distinction grounded in the supreme worth of the Son's person and deeds. Throughout the Book of Hebrews we shall need to think clearly and maintain this balancing act if we would be true to its argument.

So we arrive at the decisive word of the opening sentence. Just as the first phrase draws attention to the imperfect (incomplete) nature of the Old Testament, so the apostle, for emphasis, puts the principal term last—"Son." We have been translating the words as, "He has spoken to us by [in] a Son," but the Greek is literally "He has spoken to us in Son." The force of the construction directs attention to the *quality* of Sonship, so that we may rightly translate the passage as, "He has spoken to us in One who is Son." [14]

If "prophets" sums up the Old Testament speaking of God, "Son" embraces the New. Embraces—and gathers up all the Old, surpassing it by reason of the dignity of that name.

We need to take a hard look at the key word *Son*. The apostle comes back to it in critical places in his sermon. Every time it bears particular weight in carrying his ongoing argument.

In 1:5-14 he shows the *superiority* of Jesus to angels. We shall return to this matter later in the chapter. What interests us here is that it is because Jesus is *Son* that one must count Him better than angels, which is the force of the Old Testament quotations of verses 5-13. God never called an angel "Son" (verse 5). The Son, however, receives the designation of eternal, exalted God (verses 8-12).

The term "Son" next appears in 2:10-18. We might title the beautiful passage "The Son and the sons" (see chapter 3). We note here especially verse 11: "That is why he is not ashamed to call them brethren." Once again the reasoning points up the *exaltation* that adheres to "Son." Because He is Son, we might not expect Him to call men "brothers," but on account of the Incarnation and His human experiences, He has become our Brother.

The next reference to "Son" is unusually noteworthy. It occurs at 5:5, but only if we pick it up in context (verses 1-6) can we appreciate its full force:

"For every high priest chosen from among men is appointed to act on behalf of men in relation to God, to offer gifts and sacrifices for sins. He can deal gently with the ignorant and wayward, since he himself is beset with weakness. Because of this he is bound to offer sacrifice for his own sins as well as for those of the people. And one does not take the honor upon himself, but he is called by God, just as Aaron was.

"So also Christ did not exalt himself to be made a high priest, but was appointed by him who said to him,

" 'Thou art my Son, today I have begotten thee;' as he says also in another place, 'Thou art a priest for ever, after the order of Melchizedek.' "

Something strange has happened to the logic here. Everything is clear up to verse 5. The apostle emphasizes that no priest appoints himself. As in the case of Aaron, God calls him. So with Christ—He did not confer the priesthood upon Himself but was designated by God, who said. . . . And there is the slip. We would expect the quotation of conferral to follow: "Thou art a priest for ever, after the order of Melchizedek." But the reasoning breaks off. Instead, we find first the citation of Psalm 2:7 again—"Thou art my Son, today I have begotten thee." What has happened to the finely woven argument here?

When we look closely at the text, we observe that it ties the two Old Testament quotations together. God, designating Jesus as High Priest, first quotes Psalm 2:7. Then he adds "as he *also* says in another place," and cites Psalm 110:4. That is, *both* statements are statements of conferral. Of the two, apparently the "Son" declaration is the more significant and so appears first. *It is because Jesus is Son that God may confer the Melchizedekian high priesthood upon Him.* This finding has profound implications for the study of the priesthood of Jesus (see chapter 4).

In 6:4-6, the next reference to "Son," we again see the weight the term carries. The apostle issues his severe warning of no repentance for certain people. His key point of condemnation is that the people in view crucify afresh and hold up to public mockery *the Son of God*. They have despised what is most

42

precious, flouted the One who bears the name "Son." So no hope remains for them.

Chapter 7:3 has the next mention of "Son." We pick up the ongoing discussion at 7:1: "For this Melchizedek, king of Salem, priest of the Most High God, met Abraham returning from the slaughter of the kings and blessed him; and to him Abraham apportioned a tenth part of everything. He is first, by translation of his name, king of righteousness, and then he is also king of Salem, that is, king of peace. He is without father or mother or genealogy, and has neither beginning of days nor end of life, but resembling the Son of God he continues a priest for ever."

An interesting process of reasoning surfaces once more. Melchizedek, of course, was prior to Jesus, and we anticipate, after the strange description of verse 3a, that the apostle would conclude, "And the Son of God is like him, a priest for all time." The apostle reverses the logic, however. He does not compare the Son to Melchizedek, but Melchizedek to the Son. Once again the term "Son" carries its own supreme weight.[15]

The two other cases of "Son" parallel previous occurrences. At 7:28, the use echoes 5:5: "But the word of the oath, which came later than the law, appoints a Son who has been made perfect for ever" (again literally, "One who is Son," as in 1:2). Once more the author binds priesthood to Sonship. The second, at 10:29, duplicates the warning of 6:6. We hear repeated the stern words: "How much more severe a penalty that man will deserve who has trampled under foot the Son of God!" (NEB).

We have now looked at all the references to "Son" in Hebrews. What have we found?

—"Son" designates revelation with finality (1:2).
—"Son" indicates superiority to angels (1:5-14).
—"Son" has become our Brother (2:10-18).
—"Son" qualifies for Melchizedekian priesthood (5:5, 6; 7:28).
—Warnings are given against despising "Son" (6:6; 10:29).

Thus we may rightfully attach much importance to the Son term. As the first basis of Christian assurance is in the speaking God, so His climactic speech is One who is Son.[16] Or, we may fairly say, because of the Son we may find absolute confidence.

The ideas that center in "Son" which we have just noticed are great ones of the sermon. We shall come back to them for full consideration at the appropriate places in our study of Hebrews. But we have not yet completed our opening paragraph of Hebrews. Let us notice how it summarizes the person and work of the Son.

His Person and Work

By the "person" of the Son we mean who *He is*. The first part of 1:3 gives us an explicit statement. He "is the effulgence of God's splendour and the stamp of God's very being" (NEB).

Search through the entire New Testament and you will not find a more exalted description of Christology. Only the opening lines of the prologue of the Fourth Gospel with their majestic phraseology: "In the beginning was the Word, and the Word was with God, and the Word was God" touch the same sublime level. The statement merits close study.

We notice three aspects to it. First, the passage calls the Son the *apaugasma* of God's glory. Translated "effulgence" in the NEB, "brightness" in KJV, and "radiance" by Phillips, the word indicates "a bright ray," "a shining forth." The apostle is describing the *glory* of the Son. He is a ray from the Ineffable Splendor. As the ancient creed put it, "Light of light." We catch here a glimpse of the limitless glory attached to the person of the Son.

Second, He is the *character* of God's essence. The original Greek word, the source of our English *character,* has the idea of a stamp, an impression made in wax, a coin which bears the image of a king or president. The idea goes beyond mere appearance. The apostle tells us that the Son has the very *being* of God—what God *is,* He is.

The author does not speak of moral qualities, as we do when we use the word *character.* Rather, we should think of orders of existence. Consider, for instance, the following list: cauliflower, frog, monkey, man, God. We know well the first four terms in the series and realize that, while they have in common the principle of life, they mark ascending levels of being. The fifth term, God, we can but dimly grasp. By analogy, however, we may understand that, as a frog represents a higher order of existence than a cauliflower, and so on, so God's being surpasses ours. Eternal, self-existent, free from the processes of physical change and decay that form part of our mode of existence, His essence surpasses ours. And the Son bears that divine stamp. What God is, the Son is.

As we reflect on these sublime words—the Son as Ray of the Ineffable Splendor and Stamp of the Eternal Essence—we see how important they are for a correct conception of Jesus Christ. They put the Son on such an exalted plane that we must fall at His feet and adore Him. He is deity. Nothing less will do. Further, they force us to acknowledge eternal distinctions *within* God. Here is the value of the back-to-back illustrations of 1:3. If we had only the first, we might conclude that the Son is merely a reflection or extension of the one Divine Person. The second, however, does not allow this. Although both indicate one divine glory and essence, the second points us to a separate, personal existence of the Son within the divine splendor and being. While the passage does not mention the Holy Spirit, the language does attempt to express that mystery which the Christian church came to call "Trinity."

We have used "eternal" several times in the above paragraphs. Can we be sure that the Son eternally has been, is, and will be all that 1:3 tells us—Light of light, God of God? What about Arius in the fourth century AD (and he has modern supporters) who taught that the Son *became?* That is, that the Father *exalted* Him to the preeminent status described here, that there was a time when He was not?

The third aspect of our verse eliminates such questions. The apostle—that master of careful writing—uses the verb to be. Literally his construction reads: "The Son, . . . who *being* the effulgence of God's splendor and the stamp of God's very being." He does *not* say, as he might have if he so intended: "The Son, who *became* the effulgence of God's splendor and the stamp of

God's very being." The distinction is crucial, just as it is in John 1:1—not "the Word *became* God," but "the Word *was* God." His language, in both key passages, cut the ground out from Arius, just as it has from modern-day Jehovah's Witnesses.[17]

Now we are ready to look at the "work" of the Son. By that we mean what He *does*—past, present, future. And we might add, person and work flow together in thought just as they do in 1:2-4. That is, He does what He does because of who He is. His person is the source and value of His work, and in reflex fashion, His work brings greater honor to His person.

As we look at the work of the Son in 1:2-4, we notice that we can view it in a time sequence. We might designate it as preincarnate, incarnate, and postincarnate.

The Son's preincarnate work was Creation and providence. He was the Agent of God to create the "worlds," or, as the NEB puts it, "all orders of existence." The apostle indicates that the universe not only has its origin in God (that is, it isn't a product of chance), but that it is unified. No place for star wars here, with two eternal forces opposing each other. All that is has come from God. And the Son is the Active Person of Deity to bring it all about.

Further, He *sustains* the universe by the word of His power (1:3). The picture here is not that of Atlas burdened under the weight of the world. Instead, it is the Son whose divine word-energy activates and actualizes all that is. "He's got the whole world in His hands." He who is the Source of all that is, continually maintains all that is. Without that dynamic word, the universe would collapse into nothingness.

The apostle encompasses the Incarnation in but a fistful of words—"when he had made purification for sins" (1:3). The birth, the ministry, the exorcisms, the teachings, he gathers up in this one superlative work of the incarnate Son.

Here we find the first hint of what is to come in Hebrews. All other aspects of His work—Creation, providence, exaltation, heirship—will remain undeveloped in the sermon. This one, however, will receive great prominence. The theological argumentation as it rises to a crescendo in 9:1–10:18 will zero in on elaborating the phrase concerning purgation of sins.

The author of Hebrews emphasizes "when he *had* made purification of sins." He stresses Christ's completed, decisive, final work. And so, as the exalted person of the Son gives us assurance, so does His activity on our behalf. In Him—who He is and what He has done—we find a basis for absolute confidence.

The apostle describes the postincarnate work of the Son in terms of exaltation and heirship. Verse 3 tells us that He "sat down at the right hand of the Majesty on high," exalted far above the angels. It is a picture of triumph, of royal authority. The Son reigns in highest heaven. This session (taking His royal throne) indicates something else. It confirms the incarnate work of purging sins—when He *had* purged our sins, He *sat down.* A completed atonement here, a provision for the age-old sin problem that is altogether adequate. The apostle occasionally returns to the kingly portrayal (1:13; 8:1; 10:12). How it fits in with his primary emphasis of Jesus as heavenly High Priest must concern us later (see chapter 6).

Even though the Son now reigns as King, Hebrews calls Him "heir of all things" (1:2). How is this? It is because only heaven and the church presently acknowledge and proclaim Him as Lord. Although He made a thoroughgoing sacrifice for sins, the entire universe has not chosen to accept it. Only those who believe receive it.

But He is heir to all. In the outworking of the eternal purposes of God, the universe will at last return to the Son.

The proem of Hebrews 1:1-4 majestically opens the sermon. Its tone lifts us to the presence of God, its conceptions stagger our intellects, its throb of absolute certainty warms and gladdens our hearts. We would do well to dwell long on the words. When we have fully grasped—and been grasped—by them we shall quickly understand what follows.

While the text naturally leads to the threefold division we adopted, another is possible—the Son as Prophet, Priest, and King:

—Prophet, because He is the Supreme Revelation, the Climactic Speech of God

—Priest, because He brings about purgation of sins
—King, because He reigns at the right hand of God.
Of the three ideas, it is the middle one—Jesus as Priest—that
occupies the attention of Hebrews.

We have spent some time on the term "Son." Now we see
that we should not press the designation too far in the direction of
human analogies. When Scripture calls Jesus Son, it does *not*
mean that He has had *origin* in God: that because God generated
Him, He is His "Son." Sonship among human beings leads to
such a conclusion—but the apostle specifically denies it. The Son
has the divine being (or "nature"), just as our children share our
nature, but the Son *always* had divinity.

Nor is He "Son" because of the Incarnation. It is the *Son* who
is incarnated. At the birth He becomes "Son of God" in a special
sense, but He was eternally Son before.[18]

The ultimate meaning of *Son* here eludes us. And indeed it
must. For we are dealing with the topic of God Himself, the one
God who exists in trinitarian, personal distinctions. We may say
that the "Son language," as elsewhere in the New Testament,
points us to divine *functions* rather than to origins. As in the
Fourth Gospel, the "Father" sends the Son, gives Him words,
authority, and even life, so here the activity of God as seen by His
creatures is that of the Son who creates, sustains, purifies, reigns,
and inherits.

The Son and Angels

The final words of the proem point to the Son's superiority to
the angels. The rest of chapter 1 drives home the idea by way of
four arguments drawn from Scripture:

1. The exclusive divine name—"Son." No angel was ever
called "Son" (verse 5), but He is so addressed in Psalm 2:7 and 2
Samuel 7:14.

2. Angels are to worship Him (verse 6). The quotation here is
from the Greek translation (the Septuagint) of Deuteronomy
32:43.

3. The nature of the Son and angels contrasted

(a) Angels are "winds" and "flames of fire" (verse 7). The citation is from the Greek version of Psalm 104:4.

(b) The Son, however, is directly addressed as "God," whose throne is forever and who is exalted over all (verses 8, 9). The quotation is Psalm 45:6, 7.

(c) The Son is the Eternal, Changeless One. All else may grow old and fade away, but He is the same for all time (verses10-12). Here the apostle cites Psalm 102:25-27.

4. The service of the Son and angels contrasted

(a) No angel was ever called to reign at God's right hand (verse 13). The quotation is from Psalm 110:1.

(b) The work of the angels is that of "ministrant spirits" (NEB), sent out to serve for the sake of the people of God (verse 14).

The apostle's presentation here is fascinating. For him the word of the Old Testament is the highest authority, enough to settle debate. And that word is an arsenal of Messianic allusions, or, we might say, is Christological throughout. Even passages such as 2 Samuel 7:14, originally addressed to David, or psalms which do not appear to have Messianic reference hum with Christological significance.

As the apostle establishes the Son's superiority over angels He emerges as God. The ideas implied in 1:2, 3 now come to direct expression. Why does the apostle go to such trouble here? Surely, in view of the majestic 1:1-4, the rest of the chapter appears redundant. Was it really *necessary* to spend so much time in showing what should have been obvious, that the Son is greater than the angels?

I suggest two reasons for his concern. First, the point he makes in 1:5-14 is important for his exhortation at 2:1-4. Here he contrasts "the message declared by angels" (2:2) with the salvation "declared at first by the Lord" (2:3). The former refers to the giving of the law at Sinai, where as Galatians 3:19 puts it, angels acted as intermediaries (see also Deuteronomy 33:2). The latter refers to the giving of the gospel, spoken by the Lord Himself. That is, the apostle is showing *how much greater* is the privilege of Christians—and so, how much greater the peril of neglect. The argument is from the lesser to the greater. If the people who disobeyed at the time of Moses received punishment, how shall we think to escape if we ignore salvation so great—as greater as is the Lord than angels?

This explanation, however, does not seem sufficient in itself. Granted that the apostle *employs* the point of the Son's superiority to angels in 2:1-4, its long development in 1:5-14 calls for further explanation. Obviously there is more behind Hebrews than first meets the eye.

In chapter 1 we drew up a spiritual profile of the Hebrews. It did not, however, enable us to know what sort of strange ideas may have been current in the readers' environment. At 13:8, 9 the apostle says, without telling us what he has in mind, "Do not be swept off your course by all sorts of outlandish teachings" (NEB). Could one such idea have been the worship of angels?

We have strong evidence of great interest in angelology in the first century AD. The Christians in Colossae, we know from Paul's letter, dabbled with angel worship (see Colossians 2:18). Non-Biblical literature, especially Jewish, also indicates heightened angelic speculation and veneration. Often the concepts involved angel ministry in a heavenly sanctuary, sometimes including Melchizedek. When we consider the argument concerning Christ's high-priestly ministry (see chapter 6) we will have more to say about the subject.

It seems likely, then, that the apostle is consciously opposing a false angelology. He wants his readers to get matters straight right from the beginning: it is the *Son,* not angels, who should engage their thought and worship. While angels may have an important role to play in the service of God, they are immeasurably inferior in name, person, dignity, and function to the Son.

Absolute Confidence in the Son

The apostle's argument about the Son and angels leaves us cold. Who ever wants to put angels above Him, anyway? Yet are we in danger of worshiping "angels"—modern ones?

To many Jewish minds, an angel was the most glorious being he could imagine. (He did not dare to think of the person of Yahweh, remote in His unity.) The supernatural beings who appeared to Abram, Gideon, and Manoah, the seraphim of Isaiah's Temple vision, the living creatures of Ezekiel's theophany—they evoked wonder and admiration. During the period between the testaments the Jews identified four archangels by name—Michael, Gabriel, Raphael, and Uriel. They venerated such superbeings.

What are the most exalted "beings" for modern man? We have the "stars"—of the silver screen, of the tube, of the sports arena. They perform acts of wonder before our eyes. Clever, witty, brilliant, superb, cool, they always have the right word or the right move. They work miracles.

To be a star some day—how many people long for it! Teenagers dream, adults sigh, old age regrets. For the stars are ageless. They have discovered the fount of eternal youth, have eaten of the ambrosia of charisma.

Perhaps we need to hear again the apostle's words. Not the angels, not the stars, he tells us, but the Son! Look to Him. He is infinitely greater—in name, in Himself, in dignity.

Could it be a source of the erosion of Christian confidence in our day—that we have become modern angel-worshipers? If so, the Book of Hebrews can put us back on track.

We started this chapter by referring to the myth of Sisyphus. Here we approach the close of two thousand years since Christ, unsure of who we are and where we are going—if indeed we have anywhere to go. In our insecurity and frustration we have turned to new gods.

Hebrews will tell us that they are false gods. It will assert in ringing tones that, in the midst of our confused modern existence, we may have absolute confidence.

Our confidence does not stem from heady optimism. Nor does it derive from ideas of the inevitability of progress, of the steady evolution of the race. It is more than a personal, subjective confidence because it is based *outside* ourselves in the God who speaks.

He has cared enough to speak! Since He has always cared, He has always spoken. And then, according to His time-purpose, He spoke supremely. Jesus *Himself* became man. The Source of all, the Life of all, He entered our sin-cursed domain to share our lot. By doing so He brought us deliverance, provided purification for sins. That He now reigns in highest heaven is evidence of His all-sufficient work for us.

So, despite appearances, life is not meaningless. God is achieving an eternal purpose. The Son, God's Climactic Speech, sustains our universe, our world. That same Son will at length "inherit" all, meaning that out of the chaos, pain, doubt, and frustration will come peace and healing.

These are not merely *ideas, hopes*. They rest in *facts*, supremely in the *fact* of the Son's incarnation. Because we have heard that Speech, we may indeed find absolute confidence.

It is to that Incarnation that we now turn.

---

[1] Job 22:12, KJV.

[2] The term is from C. S. Lewis, *A Grief Observed* (Greenwich, Connecticut: Seabury Press, 1961).

[3] The attempt to establish the existence of God from rational argument occupied the philosophers for many centuries. The success of the endeavor, however, has been dubious. The classical "proofs" (the arguments from the idea of perfect being, design, or morality) are insufficient to convince the skeptic and unnecessary for the believer.

[4] Hebrews 7:21; 8:2, 8, 9, 10, 11; 10:16, 30; 12:5, 6, 14; 13:6. This derives from the apostle's use of the Septuagint. Compare occurrences of "Lord" applied to Jesus in the usual New Testament sense (Hebrews 1:10; 2:3; 7:14; 13:20).

[5] The two references to "father" at 1:5 and 12:9 are not exceptions.

[6] Hebrews 4:14; 6:6; 7:3; 10:29.

[7] Hebrews 2:4; 3:7; 6:4; 10:15, 29 (possibly 9:14 also). There appears to be a studied de-emphasis of the role of the Holy Spirit in this book.

[8] This, by the way, is true of the entire Bible. Instead of a philosophy of the person of God, God is everywhere known by what He does. For example, Genesis does not commence with the statement that God is Creator but rather shows us God actively creating.

[9] Hebrews 3:12; 9:14; 10:31; 12:22.

[10] See B. F. Westcott, *The Epistle to the Hebrews* (Grand Rapids, Michigan: Eerdmans, 1965), pp. 469-474.

[11] Hebrews 4:7 is not an exception: God speaks "through" (literally "in") David.

The Son—God's Climactic Speech

[12] Note how the subject changes from God and His speaking to the person and work of the Son as we move from verse 1 to verses 2-4.

[13] "All that man needs to know or can know of God has been revealed in the life and character of His Son. 'No man hath seen God at any time; the only-begotten Son, which is in the bosom of the Father, He hath declared Him.' John 1:18. Taking humanity upon Him, Christ came to be one with humanity and at the same time to reveal our heavenly Father to sinful human beings" (Ellen G. White, *Testimonies for the Church*, Vol. 8, p. 286).

[14] Westcott, *The Epistles to the Hebrews*, p. 7.

[15] These remarks should help us to get our friend Melchizedek in perspective. We shall come back to him in chapter 4.

[16] "The Son is all the fullness of the Godhead manifested. The Word of God declares Him to be 'the express image of His person.' . . .

"Christ is the preexistent, self-existent Son of God. . . . In speaking of His preexistence, Christ carries the mind back through dateless ages. He assures us that there never was a time when He was not in close fellowship with the eternal God. He to whose voice the Jews were then listening had been with God as one brought up with Him. . . . He was equal with God, infinite and omnipotent. . . . He is the eternal, self-existent Son. . . .

"While God's Word speaks of the humanity of Christ when upon this earth, it also speaks decidedly regarding His preexistence. The Word existed as a divine being, even as the eternal Son of God, in union and oneness with His Father" (Ellen G. White, *Evangelism*, pp. 614, 615).

[17] "In Christ is life, original, unborrowed, underived" (Ellen G. White, *The Desire of Ages*, p. 530).

[18] Note how Ellen G. White, while affirming the eternal Sonship (see note 16), suggests that the Incarnation made Him Son in a new sense: "While the Son of a human being, He became the Son of God in a new sense. Thus He stood in our world—the Son of God, yet allied by birth to the human race" (*Selected Messages*, Book One, p. 227).

Chapter 3

The Brother—
One With Us

Six hundred years before Jesus, a religious madness swept across Greece. Women made their way to the mountains and, in ceremonies of wild frenzy, tore the raw flesh of goats and devoured it. Other cults subsequently arising featured colorful processions, high drama, secret rites, initiations, and spiritual exuberance. The "mysteries" still flourished when Christianity burst on the scene, and they formed rivals to it.[1]

Why did such strange new forms of worship arise? Because of man's desire to *experience* the presence of God. In one way or another, the mysteries offered a God one could feel personally, know, even be absorbed into. The old pantheon atop Olympus—Zeus, Apollo, Hera, and so on of the *Iliad* and *Odyssey*—was remote. Absorbed in their own concerns, the gods were far removed from man in his problems and existential strivings. Hence the appeal of the mysteries.

We have seen a similar development in recent years. Under the impact of the space age, a personal God seemed ever more distant from modern man. The moon lost its magic as Americans left their imprint in the lunar dust. Recently Mars has revealed its barren and desolate face. As the first Russian cosmonauts circled

the earth they radioed back, "We haven't found God out here!"
Even some theologians jumped on the bandwagon. The "God is
dead" movement flourished during the 1960s.

But then a strange reversal occurred. Despite the wonders of
technological achievements, even in their *midst,* the late sixties
saw a turning to the occult, to Eastern religions, and to astrology.
Films like *Rosemary's Baby* and *The Exorcist* were box-office hits,
and a rash of books dealing with the weird and the supernatural
appeared. In the seventies a Christian counterpart suddenly
sprang up—the "Jesus movement" and charismatic Christianity.[2]

Whether a person intones "Hare Rama," speaks in tongues, or
asks the passerby if he is "saved," the one common factor is the
desire to *feel* God, to experience Him. Clearly, a remote God,
great though He may be, cannot long satisfy man.

Which brings us to the problem raised by our last chapter. We
saw there how *great* is God the Son. His name, His being, His
works—they stagger the mind. All that God is He is, and all that
God does He does. The Ageless One, He is clad in ineffable
majesty, seated in highest heaven.

But His very transcendence signifies His *distance* from us. Has
the apostle, seeking to show how great is the Son, actually left us
groping in our aloneness as we grasp the magnificence of His
person?

He has not. If Hebrews 1 sets forth the superlative being of the
Son, chapter 2 brings Him close to us. Side by side we find the
highest language in support of His deity and the strongest
arguments for His humanity. The Son has become the
Brother—our Brother.

The apostle wants us to be absolutely convinced of it. Indeed,
his whole argument regarding Jesus as heavenly High Priest will
crash in ruins if he cannot show the humanity. So, while he
argues most extensively for the point in 2:5-18, he comes back to
it over and over. We shall do well to follow carefully the leading
assertions that he makes:

> The fact of the Son's humanity
> The sufferings of the Son
> The temptations of the Son

The perfecting of the Son
The accomplishment of the Son's humanity
Let us take them up in order.

The Fact of Humanity

Just as the apostle explicitly attributes deity to the Son, so he directly asserts His humanity. The only difference in presentation involves that whereas Sonship is an *eternal* predication, humanity occurred in time. Or, we may say, He always *was* and *is* Son, but He *became* man. In 5:5-8 we see both ideas in sharp relief: "thou art my Son," "in the days of His flesh," "although he was a Son."

The first statement of humanity comes at 2:9: "But we see Jesus, who for a little while was made lower than the angels," argues the apostle. He has quoted from Psalm 8, which, although originally a song of the glory of man, he finds charged with Messianic import. The song tells of the "son of man" who is for a short time inferior to angels but is subsequently exalted above them—a prediction of the incarnation (humiliation) and exaltation of the Son (that is, a correspondence with 1:3b, 4).[3]

We need to go back to 1:5-14 to catch the force of the logic here. As we saw earlier, the apostle wanted to assure his readers that the Son was immeasurably better than angels, no matter how marvelous the latter beings. But someone could have objected, "Your argument is all wrong. You say Jesus is the Son and far greater than angels? But *we* know He was a man, that He suffered and even died—something that doesn't happen to angels." The apostle would have replied, "Yes, my friend, He *did* have experiences lower than angels. But they were only for a little while. For a short time He was made (became) inferior to angels, but He was subsequently exalted far above them." Here the argument is an apologetic, defensive one. Before the chapter is through we shall see how it turns into an offensive one, as the apostle will reason on behalf of the *indispensability* of the period of humanity for the accomplishment of the Son's work.

At 2:14 we find another assertion of humanity. The apostle reasons from family blood relations: "The children of a family share the same flesh and blood; and so he too shared ours" (NEB). It is an exceedingly strong statement. As 2:9 told of the Son's entering into a phase of inferiority to the angels He created and sustained, so this passage tells of His taking of actual human nature.

The most appealing argument, however, comes in 2:11-13. Two key expressions occur here—"all of one" (verse 11, NEB) and "brothers" (verses 12, 13, NEB). The first, actually *ex henos*, has had various translations: "who . . . have all one origin" (RSV), "are all of one stock" (NEB), "share a common humanity" (Phillips), and so on. Here the apostle introduces an idea that he will elaborate in 5:1-10, namely that the priest must share a common bond with his people. We may see the expression as signifying a *shared nature* (most likely) or *shared experience*. In either interpretation we see how close to us is the Son in His humanity.

Since the Son and we are "all of one," He *identifies* Himself with us. He does not feel ashamed to be called man, nor does He shrink from us. In fact, He proclaims us His brothers. Before the heavenly hosts, those legions of angels superior to us as they for a little while were superior to Him, He, the Son, King in victory and glory, calls men His brothers.

At a stroke vanishes the problem of the remote God. The high God has come close to us. And may we never forget it—come close forever. The Son, made a little while lower than angels, has become eternally the Brother of the human race.

"He had to be made like these brothers of his in every way" (2:17, NEB). We notice the great ideas of chapter 2 flowing together: (1) He becomes ("is made") human; (2) not angels, but *human beings*, become His brothers (cf verse 16); and (3) He becomes like us "in every way"—the commonality, the union of the *ex henos* of 2:11 once again.

In his direct assertions of the Son's humanity the apostle has employed the most winning analogy possible. He has argued on the basis of family blood ties—the most ancient and still the most basic of social relationships. It is in the family that we belong, that we find our *identity*, our origin, and our "world." And he tells us that Christianity is the family of God, with the Son our blood brother. Though *His* origins predate the family tree, He *became* a member—not by adoption but by birth. And though His origins place Him far outside our pale, He is not ashamed of us, but ready to proclaim to the assembled universe that we are *His* brothers.[4]

Apart from the above explicit statements of humanity, the apostle presents the *experiences* of the Son "in the days of His flesh." They are unquestionably *human* experiences as He suffers, is tested, and is perfected.

The Sufferings of the Son

No book of the Bible so starkly portrays the sufferings of Jesus as Hebrews. Only in the Synoptic accounts of the agony of Gethsemane do we approach the intensity of the apostle's sermon.

Let us make sure of one thing at the outset. When Hebrews speaks of the sufferings of Jesus, and it does in six places (2:9, 10, 18; 5:7, 8; 9:26; 13:12), there is a *spiritual* dimension involved. We will notice how often the author associates the idea of suffering with death. That is, the apostle is not addressing the general problem of human woe—our heartaches and our ailments, our tragedies and our pain. The sufferings of Jesus here are primarily mental.

Three passages demand close attention. We have already begun to look at the first one—2:9, 10. The apostle has reasoned, as we noticed above, that the Son was only temporarily lower than angels, but he goes on to state that the exaltation of the Son was on account of "the suffering of death"—the suffering associated with death.

What were His sufferings? The pangs of death so common to mankind? Certainly much more, for he tells us that Christ tasted death "for us all" (NEB). Here are vicarious sufferings, which, because Christ has already borne them, are no longer our lot. They are more than the despairing "O God, save me!" that springs to the lips of man gazing into the maw of eternal

58

nonbeing. He tasted death, drank to the bitter dregs the cup of woe from which He had pleaded to be spared—"My Father, if it be possible, let this cup pass from me; nevertheless, not as I will, but as thou wilt" (Matthew 26:39).

There is an element in the death of Christ that eludes our experience. His is more than an innocent's miscarriage of justice, far more than a martyr's. When we hear the words of desolation from the cross, "My God, my God, why hast thou forsaken me?" (Matthew 27:46), we sense the dimension of divine mystery. The Son has entered into a horror of forsakenness, of utter aloneness, that we cannot comprehend. In theological terminology He suffered the "second death."[5] And, says the apostle, "for us all."

We must notice yet one more point in 2:9. While most manuscripts of the Greek text read: "the suffering of death, so that *by the grace of God* He might taste death for every one," a few extremely early ones read "so that, *apart from God,* He might taste death for us all." The difference in the Greek involves a change of but two letters of the Greek alphabet. The two meanings, however, stand in strong contrast.

In my judgment the majority vote is wrong here. After all, one old manuscript has more significance than twenty or fifty later ones. Further, the reading "apart from God" is obviously the more difficult one to accept theologically. We can understand how a copyist could have changed it into "by the grace of God," but not *vice versa.*

When we read 2:9 the stark poignancy of the portrayal immediately strikes us. The Son, who had become a little while lower than angels, suffers *alone.* In the utter desolation of the cross, He tastes death—He experiences its bitterness, its horror. And He does it, not for Himself, but *for us!*[6]

The apostle stresses the *genuineness* of the Son's human experiences. No make-believe here, no grand design whose outcome is assured so that the cross is a mere formality, a stage in the divine plan. Instead, we observe risk, struggle, suffering—suffering of an order which we can but dimly comprehend. Is such a grim picture the intent of the apostle in Hebrews?

The second passage, 5:7-10, makes it clear that he has exactly that in mind. "In the days of his flesh, Jesus offered up prayers and supplications, with loud cries and tears, to him who was able to save him from death, and he was heard for his godly fear. Although he was a Son, he learned obedience through what he suffered; and being made perfect he became the source of eternal salvation to all who obey him, being designated by God a high priest after the order of Melchizedek."

The language, strong in the English translations, is even more graphic in the original. It depicts urgent and intense supplication. *Deēsis* and *hiketēria* alike indicate request, entreaty, even begging, while the pleas come with "loud cries and tears." The scene, which surely refers to the Gethsemane experience of Jesus, goes beyond the Gospel accounts in its vividness. Nowhere else in the Bible do we find such a picture of the *dependence* of Jesus, of the revulsion of His being from the prospect of death.

Once again the death motif appears. Christ urgently asks the Father to deliver Him from death. He directs His pleas to the One who is *able* to save Him from the impending experience, the One in whose will the entire universe and its history exist.[7]

The contrast with our study in the previous chapter is profound. Note how 5:8 recognizes it—"although he was a Son" or better, "son though he was" (NEB). We find no suggestion that, because of the Incarnation, Jesus has in some way lost deity. He remains the Son—but, because of humanity, a self-limitation operates that ensures His experiences as a man are genuine, starkly and terribly real. So He who made all things and upholds all and gives life to all has become a suppliant, beseeching God to rescue Him from the horror of death of the cross.

We may note a third passage—12:1-11. True, it does not employ the actual vocabulary of suffering, but the context indicates parallels with 2:9, 10 and 5:7-10. Verses 2 through 4 focus on the Son's cross as He engages the struggle with sin to the ultimate point of giving His life: "Looking to Jesus the pioneer and perfecter of our faith, who for the joy that was set before him endured the cross, despising the shame, and is seated at the right hand of the throne of God.

"Consider him who endured from sinners such hostility against himself, so that you may not grow weary or fainthearted. In your struggle against sin you have not yet resisted to the point of shedding your blood."

The apostle here speaks of the disgrace of the cross, a despised instrument, feared and abhorred throughout the Roman Empire. The authorities reserved it for noncitizens and the worst offenders. And, as the gospel records inform us, actual insults and personal abuses, shouts of derision and mockery, accompanied Jesus' crucifixion (see Matthew 27:24-44).

The apostle uses a significant preposition in verse 2—*anti*. Its meaning is similar to our modern use of *anti*—"instead of," "in the place of." That is, Jesus, in the place of all the joy of His position as heavenly Son, chose to endure the cross with its calumny (rather than the idea that He endured the cross *for the sake of* the joy at its end).[8] As 13:12 puts it so well, He suffered "outside the gate"(NEB)—outside the sacred environs, apart from the circle of religious ritual, in an unhallowed place—a place of desecration.

It is difficult for us to appreciate the theology of suffering of the New Testament. Fed the pleasure principle so long, we cannot accept the concept of redemptive suffering.[9] The Book of Hebrews, however, may open our ears once more to hear—if we spend time long enough with it. When we catch its seriousness in setting forth the sufferings of Jesus, we will have no doubt as to the genuineness of the full humanity of Jesus Christ.

The Temptations of the Son

Only two passages of Hebrews specifically mention the temptations of the incarnate Son. Explicit, however, they have captured the attention of Christians throughout the centuries. They frequently surface in discussions of the Christian life today.

The first is at 2:18—"Because he himself has suffered and been tempted, he is able to help those who are tempted." Here the apostle makes the point about Christ's qualifications to be our high priest. His ability to help the tempted ones stems from His own experiences of having been tempted. Clearly, at the very least, we may assume the *reality* of Jesus' temptations. The argument is "since . . . therefore." If it had been impossible for Him to fail, if His temptations were only an illusion, how could He succor us in ours—for we know ours are real.

A word of caution in vocabulary may help us. The word for "temptation" here, as elsewhere in the New Testament, has the essential idea of *testing*. It is a broader idea, a more positive one, than the dreary, sin hang-up stereotype of current Christian usage. The NEB translates 2:18, "Since he himself has passed through the test of suffering, he is able to help those who are meeting their test now."

Note the sort of "help" that the apostle has in mind. It is *victorious* help—not encouragement for those who have succumbed to the test (though he probably would not deny this), but fortitude to endure the test, as the Son in the days of His flesh endured.

The second statement occurs at 4:15, 16: "For we have not a high priest who is unable to sympathize with our weaknesses, but one who in every respect has been tempted as we are, yet without sin. Let us then with confidence draw near to the throne of grace, that we may receive mercy and find grace to help in time of need."

First, in a literal translation, Christ was "tempted (tested) in everything according to likeness." Here the suggestion of similarity of experience implicit in the 2:18 assertion receives emphatic expression. The reference to "likeness" we should most probably link with the ideas of 2:10, 14, where, as we saw, the author underlines the human *nature* of the Son. That is, the apostle declares that Jesus, because of His nature in common with ours, has been tempted in everything.

Second, His tests were *in all things,* or *in every way.* The apostle excludes any suggestion that Christ's temptations were temporary, limited, or confined to the wilderness or Gethsemane experiences. He wishes to show the *closeness* of Jesus to man. The apostle leaves no doubt as to the commonality of Jesus' tests with ours.

Third, He was *without sin* throughout the tests. Despite the heat of the temptations, despite their variety, He remained steadfast throughout. He endured every test.

Bishop Westcott in his commentary on Hebrews reminds us that the one who falls never knows the full force of temptation, since he fails before the test ends. So Jesus is the only one who has ever lived who has known the extremity of temptations, for only He stayed "without sin" throughout. Temptation at length succumbed to Him, not He to it.[10]

Thus, fourth, the sympathy of which the apostle speaks is not a sharing in our common fallenness but an understanding of our struggles. Because *He* endured, He knows our trials, our efforts to endure.

Finally, the "timely help" of verse 16 (NEB) is *overcoming* help. As in 2:18, the apostle does not so much deal with forgiveness for the fallen as he sets out Jesus, the One who provides strength to endure victoriously.

The Book of Hebrews leaves some of our questions about Jesus, the Son incarnate in the midst of struggle, unanswered. We may wonder, for instance, how Jesus could be tested in everything or in all ways, when our twentieth-century way of life is so different from His. The point, perhaps, is not in a *listing* of our "temptations" (again, along the lines of our preoccupation with "sin") as in the enduring of the *tests* of life. To Jesus as to us, the Christian life calls for a series of decisions. They all center in the will of God and amount to: Will I be *loyal* to my God, despite the pressures? In this respect His temptations forever remain a pattern of ours.

More difficult is the issue over the nature of Jesus. The apostle clearly argues for the genuine, full humanity of Jesus. But does he support the "sinful" or "sinless" nature of Christ? Can we reason back from his statements in 2:18 and 4:15 and detect which side he supports?

In my judgment it is invalid to use Hebrews in such a debate. The problem is that the New Testament writers were not conscious of the distinction between "sinful" and "sinless" natures and so did not address it.[11] *We* may be agitated over it,

63

but not they. For them it was sufficient to affirm the reality of the Son's humanity and His testing, the certainty of His sinlessness throughout all temptations, and His ability to help the Christian to overcome in the hour of his testing.

The Perfecting of the Son

Three times Hebrews sets forth a mind-boggling idea—that the incarnate Son was "perfected":

2:10—He was made "perfect through suffering."

5:9—When He became perfect, He "became the source of eternal salvation."

7:28—The Son was "made perfect for ever."

What is the nature of the Son's perfecting? We may discount at once two possible interpretations.

First, it could not mean an *adoptionistic* Christology, that is, that God *raised* Jesus to the level of a divine status that He did not have before. A number of people in the early centuries of the Christian church advocated such positions, that the man Jesus at a point in time such as the baptism or the ascension was elevated to a place of dignity, which we have already seen in Hebrews. But the apostle's words deny such a view. We remember the "being" of 1:2, 3 ("one who is Son, who *being*," not "became"), while 5:7-9 and 7:28, which speak of His perfecting, call Him "Son" *during* the perfecting. That is, He is not a man or superior being who, because of His earthly perfecting, becomes qualified to be Son. Rather, it is *the* Son, *while* Son, who is perfected.

Second, the perfecting does not signify a work of purifying the Son's humanity. The apostle does not set forth Jesus' experience "in the days of his flesh" as a progressive overcoming of sins in Himself. Rather, the sermon unequivocally contrasts the sinfulness of common man with His undefiled person:

4:15—Though tested in every way, He remained "without sin."

5:3, 9—The moral weakness of the Aaronic priests finds no counterpart in Him.

7:26—He is termed "holy, blameless, unstained."

7:27—He had no need to offer up sacrifices on His own behalf, as did the Aaronic priests.

9:14—He offered Himself as a sacrifice "without blemish" to God.

The context gives us the clue to grasping the intent of Hebrews in the language of the Son's "perfecting." We note that both 2:10 and 5:8, 9 speak of perfecting through *suffering,* while all three relate the perfecting work to His role as *high priest* (see 2:17, 18; 5:9, 10; 7:27, 28). The "perfecting" describes the successive experiences of the incarnate Son, experiences that led Him into new levels of dependence on God and so qualified Him to be our High Priest.

Perhaps our concept of perfection has been one sided. We may be so concerned with the struggle to overcome sin that we automatically equate perfection with sinlessness. But let us think about that for a moment. Such a view is altogether inadequate. "Sinlessness" designates merely an *absence.* It lacks positive content. Is not perfection rather a state of wholeness, of completeness, wherein we reflect the fullness of the love and beauty of God, who is the Holy (whole) One?[12]

The "perfecting" of the Son, then, indicates a *learning* process. Often our learning in the school of life proceeds by way of our mistakes. Our failures teach us wisdom and understanding of ourselves and our environment. Not so with Jesus. He learned, not by falling and rising up to overcome the next time, but by continual submission to the will of God.

Submission is progressive. As we learn to give ourselves to the Divine Self, He leads us into new levels of understanding of His plan and His ways. Here we find the meaning of the Christian's "reconversion" every day.[13] We become more like Him, we grasp new insights into His Word, we draw ever closer in our relationship to Him. So real does He become to us that we feel we hardly knew Him at all when we first became Christians.

So with Jesus. He was ever learning anew the meaning of conformity to the divine will as the experiences of life unfolded. It was as that will challenged Him to *act* that submission brought suffering. But He went forward, constantly working out in Himself the divine plan, never turning from it no matter what its cost. The final test was the ultimate one. In the Garden He cried out with loud shouts and tears. But even there He went forward—forward to the cross!

Sufferings, temptations, and perfecting—they form a theological trio that points unerringly toward genuine humanity. The apostle tells us that just as His *nature* was in common with ours, so were His *experiences*. He knew the depths of anguish, the fires of test, the successive and progressive yielding of His all into the divine will. He *was* (as He *is*) the Son. But as a man He *became*—*became* a sufferer, *became* a suppliant, *became* a dependent, *became* a learner. So, by what He went through—*because* He went through—He was "perfected." His human experiences—intense, real, genuine—made Him complete for the heavenly work of high priest that the divine plan had ordained.

The Accomplishment of Humanity

We noticed how the apostle in 2:5-8 answers the implied objection that the Son was inferior to angels because of His humanity. He argues that it was *only for a little while* that the Son stooped lower than angels.

The author of Hebrews feels no need to apologize for the Son's humanity. Far from it! He goes on to argue in the second chapter and later that the humanity is *indispensable* for the work that the divine will ordained. Three principal accomplishments emerge directly from His humanity—His vicarious death, His deliverance from the tyranny of the threat of nonbeing, and His qualifying to be a high priest.

He tasted death "for every one" (2:9). Here we observe the first direct benefit of His humanity. True, no angel had ever had to die. Certainly none had entered the horrors of the dark chamber of Gethsemane-Calvary. But no angel, likewise, had been able to help man, doomed to eternal separation from God. It was the Son alone who tasted the eternity of nothingness, who could bring hope. His agony of separation was not on His own account. It was vicarious—"for [on behalf of] every one."

In 2:14, 15, the poignancy of the language strikes answering chords in each reader. He is a picture of Everyman, whether first or twentieth century. Everyman is a slave, a prisoner of the devil, living life in the bondage of the fear of death.

Our minds run back to that Roman world into which Jesus was born, to its tombstones with their pitiful inscriptions: "Goodbye, my friend. I'll never see you again. . . . Farewell, dear Alexamenos. . . . Alas, my friend." And they run forward to the literature of our day, to the despair and frustration of writers like Kafka, Sartre, and Hemingway as they face "the dirty joke" [14] of a life that ebbs away into eternal emptiness.

The second accomplishment of the Son's humanity was to liberate man from his existential fear. "The children of a family share the same flesh and blood; and so he too shared ours, *so that through death* he might break the power of him who had death at his command, that is, the devil; and might liberate those who, through fear of death, had all their lifetime been in servitude" (2:14, 15, NEB). The Son became man *so that He might die,* says the apostle. He would enter the enemy's ground and subject Himself to the terrors of the supreme, the eternal, weapon. But by so doing, He would turn the tables on the ancient enemy. Taking the devil's instrument, He would nullify it. Just as He tasted death for every man, assuming our place before God, so by His own experience in death He removed its terrors forevermore for those who accept Him.

The third accomplishment receives the major emphasis in the sermon. His becoming "one" with us (2:11), His sharing of our flesh and blood (2:14) and our experiences of suffering, temptation, and perfecting (2:10, 17, 18; 5:7-9; 12:2-4), lead to the point of supreme interest for the apostle. *They enabled Him to become our high priest.* We observe two aspects here: (1) His *person,* wherein humanity is a prerequisite for high priesthood (2:17, 18; 4:14-16; 5:1-10) and (2) His *sacrifice,* which as high priest He offers to God (2:17; 7:27; 8:3; 9:1-10,18). The following two chapters will examine each in detail.

The humanity of Jesus can cause no embarrassment. It is as

essential as His Sonship. Without it we must each taste the horror of the "second death," we would live in terror of eternal nonbeing, we could have no heavenly high priest. It is the humanity of the Son that grounds our absolute confidence.

Thus, the curious expression that the apostle employs becomes understandable. In 2:10 he writes of what is "fitting" for God. It is the only statement of its kind in the entire New Testament—man does not question what God ought or ought not do! But the apostle says that it "befitted" or "became" God to make the Captain of our salvation perfect through suffering. At 2:17 we find a parallel idea, if not so strong. "He *had to* be made like his brethren in every respect." Now we see the humanity of the Son, that period of His temporary inferiority to angels, placed in the context of that eternal plan which would succor man cast down in sin and existential slavery.

We catch only a glimpse of the mind of God here. Perhaps we have wanted to ask, "Was there no other way? Could not God have delivered us out of the human predicament by some other means?" The apostle tells us only that what God did was "befitting" of Him. The plan whereby the Son would take on flesh and blood, share our woe, and so deliver us accorded with what God is.[15] Going beyond his words but not, perhaps, the apostle's intent, we could say, "The God who has always spoken would speak supremely by becoming enfleshed. As His word of old brought healing in its train, so Jesus, His Speech, would win eternal liberation for all who accept Him."

Unanswered Questions

In two places (3:1 and 12:1-4) the writer exhorts the Hebrews to "consider," or look to, Jesus. But what did he have in mind?

For centuries people, believers and unbelievers alike, have puzzled over Jesus, whom Christians confess as Christ and Lord. The question of the ages is, "Who do you say that I am?" (see Matthew 16:15). Is He really, as the first believers affirmed and the church has continued to claim, *God* in the flesh? But if so, *how* can it be? How could God enter into human experience, the

Limitless into the limited, the Unconditioned into the conditioned? How could God die on the cross, for instance? Were the temptations of Jesus a reality or only an appearance?

Controversy racked the church of the first five centuries. A group of teachings emphasized the deity of Jesus to the denigration or exclusion of humanity. His humanity was but a shell or appearance, or the divine in Him overruled the human, and so on. Another group took the opposite side, so pointing up humanity that it compromised deity—the man Jesus was adopted as God's Son, and so on.

And here is the sermon to the Hebrews. It directly affirms deity, just as it emphatically declares humanity. But how could it be? The apostle does not attempt an answer. He gives us no hint of any kenotic theory (that deity was in some way emptied or laid aside for the Incarnation). Hebrews does not tell us *when* the moment of divine-human blend occurred or provide us any insight into the will of Jesus. (Did the divine will have to overcome the reluctance of a human will?) Nor does the writer of Hebrews venture to explain what happened to deity at the moment of death on the cross.

Instead we find that the preexistent Son, to whom Hebrews ascribes deity of person and work, becomes fully man, entering upon human experiences and dependent upon God. His is a humanity that suffers, is perfected, and dies.

Thus the call to "consider" Jesus is not a challenge to philosophical debate. The apostle does not deal with metaphysics but with spiritual truth. He invites us to reflect on the person of Jesus *as* Son and man—not to work out *how* He could be both.

We need to remind ourselves of something here. While theology asks questions, and must do so, let us be sure they are valid questions. At the heart of our religion lies a mystery—a mystery that will forever elude the human mind. For—and is not this our claim, both anciently and now the offense of the cross—in encountering Jesus of Nazareth we confront God Himself![16]

As we close our consideration of the Son who became our Brother, another area of questioning remains. With the apostle's stress on the sufferings, temptations, and perfecting of Jesus, the query arises: "To what extent does Hebrews point to Christ as our example?" The apostle does not directly address the issue, but his presentation allows us to draw some inferences.

First, the book lacks the idea of *imitating* Jesus. The apostle calls on his hearers to be "imitators of those who through faith and patience inherit the promises" (6:12) and points to their leaders (13:7). Negatively, he cites the disobedient Israelites as an example (4:11). In the roll call of the heroes of faith (ch. 11) he does not mention Jesus. Of course the apostle has held Him up before them in 12:2-4, but not in such a way as to draw attention to His humanity. Rather, the designation "pioneer and perfecter of our faith" suggests a qualitative distinction from us.

Second, we do not find exhortations where they would be most effective to point to Jesus as the Example, if the apostle so intended. We saw above how 2:5-18 and 5:7-10 vividly describe the struggles of the incarnate Son. Calls to follow His example could powerfully accompany such passages, but we do not find them. Instead, the practical application that follows is in terms of the *help* He can give us in our test. "He is able to help" "in time of need" and is "the source of eternal salvation" (2:18; 4:16; 5:9).

Thus, in my judgment, the great concern of Hebrews with Jesus' genuine humanity is to establish His high priesthood, not to present Him in an exemplary role. That is, the book summons us to *trust* what He has done rather than to *do* what He did.

The Brother and Us

We need to let the apostle's emphasis on the full humanity of Jesus soak through our Christian consciousness. It will give us a new understanding of our Lord and enrich our living.

The first Christians had no doubt that Jesus of Nazareth was human. No one ever came up to Him and pinched His arm, saying, "Are you for real, or is it only an appearance?" Those who saw Him and knew Him firsthand wouldn't have dreamed of questioning His humanity.

In the first century the issue was just the opposite—was He *more* than a man? All who knew Him agreed that He was human, but Christians claimed more for Him. Throughout the New Testament we see how they struggle to depict that "moreness." In Hebrews, as in John 1, that expression reaches its clarity and zenith in the attribution of deity to the man Jesus.

But the centuries have brought many changes in Christian thinking about Jesus. We now look back to the gospel stories about Him through the creeds of orthodoxy that laid down deity as the first affirmation. Whereas the people of the first century started with humanity and went on from there to affirm or deny deity, we tend to begin with deity.

I fear that many Christians have lost sight of the genuineness of Jesus' humanity. The concept of deity overshadows all so that they view the temptations as cut-and-dried, the ministry predetermined and assured, even the cross a foregone conclusion. In short, while they mouth Jesus' manhood, their concept is at best a diluted one. Jesus is a Cosmic Superman, one who can call to His aid powers and privileges that would make Clark Kent green (or blue?) with envy.

Theologically and spiritually, we have lost much. The reality of *struggle,* of *test,* of *risk*—all have blurred. We have a Jesus who is not unlike the *avataras* of Hinduism—like Rama or Krishna, who while appearing manlike, at any moment transform themselves into the lord of the universe.[17]

So the *closeness* of Jesus is lost. He is wonderful, but in a remote, other-worldly way. While great, powerful, wise, supreme, He is far from us.

We need to see again the Son as our Brother. Thus the apostle portrays Him—dependent, praying, *needing* to pray, supplicating, crying out, agonizing. Then we will realize how real and how near to us His humanity is.

Dr. Frank Boreham, a great preacher and writer, related in one of his books an experience from his early ministry. In South New Zealand, where he had just taken up his parish, he encountered an old Christian named David. David had a problem. "Pastor, I'm embarrassed to tell you. Every night when I

71

kneel to pray I fall asleep before the Lord. What can I do about it?"

Boreham thought for a moment and replied, "David, you don't have to always kneel in prayer. Why don't you try putting a chair beside yours and speak to the Lord as though He were sitting right next to you?" The old man tried it out and delighted in the new meaning he found in prayer (and no longer did he fall asleep). At length he grew feeble and was confined to bed. But always—so the pastor noticed—he kept a special chair by the bedside. It was his prayer chair. The Lord sat there, and no visitor could use it.

One day David's daughter sent an urgent call to the minister. "Come quickly! Father is sinking." But it was too late—he knew as he met her at the door that David had gone to his rest. Then she said, "When I went in to see him and found he was gone, do you know what I saw? His hand was stretched out, touching *the chair*. You understand, don't you?"

Even so may the Son, He who became our Brother, draw near to us. An appreciation of His full humanity may lead to a new understanding of the Gospel accounts and a new and closer walk with Him. A sense of His humanity will lead to absolute confidence in Him.

We move on to consider the preeminent accomplishment of that humanity—His qualifying to be heavenly high priest.

---

[1] The early "mysteries" were the Eleusinian and Dionysian mysteries. Later ones centered in the worship of Cybele, Attis, Osiris, Isis, Mithra, etc. The "mysteries" were prominent from the seventh century BC to the fourth century AD.

[2] The fascination with the occult on earth has a celestial counterpart. Witness the popularity of *Star Trek, Star Wars,* and *Close Encounters of the Third Kind.*

[3] In my judgment the term "son of man" is the key term in interpreting Hebrews 2:5-7. The apostle sees the words of Psalm 8:4-6 as a prediction of the "lowering" and subsequent "exalting" of the Son. This understanding is to be preferred to the one that sees the passage as a prediction of Messiah's fulfilling the original purpose for man.

[4] The New Testament elsewhere employs the family analogy, although not with the same penetration as here. For example, see Romans 8:15-17; Galatians 4:5-7.

⁵The actual term "second death" appears only in the Book of Revelation (2:11; 20:6, 14; 21:8). The idea, however, has Old Testament roots and widespread New Testament support.

⁶Cf. the chapter "Gethsemane" in Ellen G. White, *The Desire of Ages,* pages 685-697.

⁷The exegesis of Hebrews 5:7 presents many problems. In particular, how are we to understand the phrase "and he was heard," since the Father did *not* deliver Jesus from the death experience? The apostle's chief idea, surely, is that Jesus *needed* to be heard—thus showing his dependency "in the days of his flesh."

⁸Understood this way, the verse parallels Hebrews 5:8—"son though he was" (NEB). The NEB in a footnote acknowledges this interpretation: "who, in place of the joy that lay ahead of him."

⁹1 Peter is the preeminent New Testament document of suffering.

¹⁰Westcott, *The Epistle to the Hebrews,* p. 59.

¹¹Only two verses of the New Testament directly address the issue of the "nature" of Christ: Romans 8:3 and Philippians 2:7. Each verse, however, is ambiguous; so proponents of both sides use both in the debate!

¹²Note how a famous verse, Matthew 5:48, "You, therefore, must be perfect, as your heavenly Father is perfect," sums up the examples of "better righteousness" in Matthew 5:20-47. Each example describes *positive* conduct, especially in the area of human relations.

¹³"Our brethren should understand that self needs to be humbled and brought under the control of the Holy Spirit. The Lord calls upon those of us who have had great light to be converted *daily.* This is the message I have to bear to our editors and to the presidents of all our conferences. We must walk in the light while we have the light, lest darkness come upon us" (Ellen G. White, *Selected Messages,* Book one, p. 165).

¹⁴The term is Ernest Hemingway's. See his *A Farewell to Arms* (New York: Charles Scribner's, 1957).

¹⁵Professor F. F. Bruce has an excellent comment on this point: "There are many who are ready to tell us confidently what would and what would not be worthy of God; but in fact the only way to discover what is a worthy thing for God to do is to consider what God has actually done. The man who says, 'I could not have a high opinion of a God who would (or would not) do this or that,' is not adding anything to our knowledge of God; he is simply telling us something about himself. We may be sure that all that God does is worthy of Himself, but here our author singles out one of God's actions and tells us that 'it became him'—that it was a fitting thing for Him to do. And what was that? It was His making Jesus, through His sufferings, perfectly qualified to be the Savior of His people. It is in the passion of our Lord that we see the very heart of God laid bare; nowhere is God more fully or more worthily revealed as God than when we see Him 'in Christ reconciling the world unto himself' (2 Cor. 5:19)" (F. F. Bruce, *The Epistle to the Hebrews* [Grand Rapids, Michigan: Wm. B. Eerdmans, 1964], pp. 42, 43).

[16] "The humanity of the Son of God is everything to us. It is the golden chain that binds our souls to Christ, and through Christ to God. This is to be our study. Christ was a real man; He gave proof of His humility in becoming a man. Yet He was God in the flesh. When we approach this subject, we would do well to heed the words spoken by Christ to Moses at the burning bush, 'Put off thy shoes from off thy feet, for the place whereon thou standest is holy ground' (Ex. 3:5). We should come to this study with the humility of a learner, with a contrite heart. And the study of the incarnation of Christ is a fruitful field, which will repay the searcher who digs deep for hidden truth" (Ellen G. White, *Selected Messages,* Book one, p. 244).

[17] Cf. the transformations of Krishna in the *Bhagavadgita*.

Chapter 4

The Priest– Sympathetic Mediator

After seven chapters of theological argumentation, the apostle sums them up, "Now this is my main point: just such a high priest we have, and he has taken his seat at the right hand of the throne of Majesty in the heavens, a ministrant in the real sanctuary, the tent pitched by the Lord and not by man" (8:1, 2, NEB).

By his own words, then, the high priesthood of Jesus Christ is the central idea of Hebrews. Yet that idea is not readily accessible or appealing to modern man.

For a start, we have little to do with priests, temples, and sacrifices. In some parts of the world such ideas still have meaning. The people of India even yet offer goats to the bloodthirsty Kali in her temple in Calcutta. Brahmans preside over the temple complexes—some of them vast, highly organized, and fabulously wealthy. Shamans propitiate African deities with bloody sacrifices. But for us, in the West, especially if we are Protestant, the priestly concept is remote. Far too long we have lived on the Reformation's principle of the priesthood of believers. We have become individualized in the modern era. Even the Israelite role of the priest—somewhat of consecrated butcher—leaves us cold as we wonder at the vast outpouring of Old Testament blood.[1]

The reasoning concerning priesthood in Hebrews is complex. When people want to cite an example of obscure Biblical logic, they often refer to the Melchizedek passage of Hebrews 7. The casual reader, starting out with good intentions to master the Book of Hebrews, rarely survives to make the point of 8:1, 2.

It is our contention that the priestly argumentation of Hebrews is both understandable and valuable to Christians today. We should remember that Hebrews is a sermon, not a piece of cryptic writing, that the original readers surely grasped. While it does call for concentration on our part, we may understand its essential meaning. Our last two chapters have prepared us to see how deity and humanity flow together in the concept of priesthood. And as we recognized how deity and humanity alike are vital for Christian life, so we shall learn how priesthood gives us a third basis of absolute confidence.

We shall study the apostle's priestly argumentation in order. It centers in three sets of comparison and contrast: Jesus and Moses; Jesus and Aaron; and Jesus and Melchizedek.

Jesus and Moses

The first mention of priesthood occurs at 2:17—"Therefore he had to be made like his brethren in every respect, so that he might become a merciful and faithful high priest in the service of God, to make expiation for the sins of the people." Apparently the discussion of Jesus' deity (chapter 1) and then His humanity (chapter 2) has been leading up to this conclusion.

It is worth noting that the term "high priest" drops without explanation. Indeed, throughout Hebrews the apostle does not seek to *prove* that Jesus is high priest but rather to establish *what sort of* high priest He is. The point in itself is intriguing, although we may not sense it as such because of our familiarity with the idea of Jesus as high priest. But that familiarity comes from Hebrews. Only as we realize that *nowhere* else does the New Testament explicitly call Jesus high priest do we sense that there is more here than meets the eye. At the very least, we may conclude that the unstudied way of introducing the term "high priest" of Jesus suggests that the readers already were familiar with it. That is, the apostle had picked up an idea known to his readers, elaborated on it, and directed it to serve the practical ends of his sermon.

The verse also tells us that Jesus *became* high priest. Indeed, it was only because He was made like His brothers in all respects that He could become high priest. So we may not speak of an eternal high priesthood of Jesus. When, as we shall presently see, the apostle speaks of Him as "priest for ever," it cannot indicate a priesthood that predates the Incarnation. The humanity of the Son is prerequisite to priesthood.

The verse specifies two characteristics of Jesus as high priest—merciful and faithful. The apostle elaborates both traits in the two following passages dealing with priesthood, but in reverse order: 3:1-6 takes up the faithfulness of Jesus, while 4:14-5:10 considers His mercifulness. Let us look closely at 3:1-6.

Just as the Son is superior to angels, so now we see Him to be greater than Moses. In the process of *opposing* him to Jesus, the Book of Hebrews does not downgrade Moses as some Christian writers attempt. Rather, the apostle shows both similarity and dissimilarity.

One quality binds both Moses and Jesus—faithfulness. Moses was *like Jesus* in his steadfastness to the service of God. "He was faithful to him who appointed him, just as Moses also was faithful in God's house" (3:2). (Note how Hebrews makes comparisons against the Son and His ministry and sets chronological considerations aside. The book follows this pattern throughout.)

But Moses was also *inferior* to the Son. Verse 3 specifically states, "Jesus has been counted worthy of as much more glory than Moses," and the following verses point out three reasons: (1) Moses was only a servant, but Jesus was a son (verses 5, 6); (2) Jesus was the founder of the household (household = the economy of the people of God), while Moses was but part of the household (verse 3; notice also the use of the prepositions "in" for Moses and "over" for Jesus in verses 2, 5, 6); and (3) Moses was a witness to the words that God would speak, but the Son was Himself the Climactic Speech of God (verse 5).

The figure of Moses surfaces several times in Hebrews.[2] The apostle has little interest in him, however, introducing him principally because of his role in the old covenant laws and cultus. Instead of Moses, Hebrews focuses on the person and work of the Son, who was *faithful*—and so qualified to be our high priest.

How do "faithfulness" and "high priesthood" cohere? The connection is not as apparent as mercifulness. Yet 2:17 directly links the humanity of the Son with His *becoming* a faithful high priest, and 3:1 picks up the point. Indeed, the latter verse uses a term unique in the New Testament, as it calls Jesus "apostle." The word has the idea of commissioning, sending, ambassadorial service.

The picture that emerges is the Great Condescension. Here is the Son, Founder of the people of God, but because of the divine plan, become the Sent One for God's people. Jesus, who would send out the Twelve in His name, first was sent in His Father's name.[3] He who would challenge them, and every Christian, to be steadfast, Himself endured to the end. By His own faithfulness as a man He can exhort us to faithfulness.

And so He may *become* High Priest. Here we catch a glimpse of the apostle's deep concern to show how preciously near the Son is to us. We may count on Him as our Heavenly Mediator because He *really* endured as a man. If His experiences were not genuine, were but partial or minor, we could not trust Him to come to our aid in the hour of our need. But *in* all, *through* all, He proved faithful—and so we may know that He *understands,* He *cares,* He *can help.* The Sent One, the One faithful on earth, has thus qualified Himself to be our faithful High Priest.

Jesus and Aaron

As the comparison with Moses points up Jesus as faithful high priest, so that with Aaron highlights His mercy. "For ours is not a high priest unable to sympathize with our weaknesses. . . . Let

78

us therefore boldly approach the throne of our gracious God, where we may receive mercy and in his grace find timely help," writes the apostle (4:15, 16, NEB).

The following paragraph, 5:1-10, elaborates the concept. It falls into two parts: 1-4, which describes the characteristics of the Aaronic high priests, and 5-10, which applies them (in part) to Christ as high priest.

Seven features emerge in the discussion of the Aaronic high priests in 1-4:

1. "Chosen from among men" (verse 1), i.e., *human origin*
2. "Appointed"; "called by God" (verses 1, 4), i.e., *divine choice*
3. "Act on behalf of men" (verse 1), i.e., *representative service*
4. "Offer gifts and sacrifices" (verse 1), i.e., *cultic* service
5. "For sins" (verse 1), i.e., *atoning* service
6. "Deal gently with the ignorant and wayward" (verse 2), i.e., *sympathetic* service
7. "Offer sacrifice for his own sins" (verse 3), i.e., *sin-weakened* service

The account of the earthly high priesthood given here is an idealized one. Indeed, there exists no explicit passage in the Old Testament that sets out all the points, and nowhere does it state the particular feature of sympathy as a requirement in Old Testament times. Nor does the record of Israel's priests in the Old Testament set them out as paragons of sympathy. While many high priests probably did indeed "deal gently" with the sinners of ancient times, we know of others who certainly did not—the immoral and self-serving sons of Eli (see 1 Samuel 2:12-17); Pashur, who opposed Jeremiah (see Jeremiah 20:1-6); and Amaziah, who could not bear to hear the rebuke of Amos (Amos 7:10-17). Nor could the apostle look to recent Jewish ecclesiastical history to prove his point. The Hasmoneans, who held the high priestly office from 142 to 63 BC,[4] were embroiled in political concerns, being secular rulers as well as religious leaders, while the Sadducees of the Gospel accounts opposed Jesus and were jealous of office.[5]

The apostle does not develop a point-by-point comparison with Jesus as high priest in 5:5-10. Only two out of the seven characteristics interest him—those of the divine appointment and sympathetic service. Just as no Aaronic priest could designate himself to the sacerdotal office, so the Son did not thrust Himself forward, but was appointed as priest by the divine word of Psalm 110:4: "Thou art a priest for ever, after the order of Melchizedek" (verses 5, 6). [We shall look more closely at this Old Testament prediction in the next section.] And just as the Aaronite priests were, according to the idealized account of 5:1-4, beset with weakness and conscious of the fact, so the Son learned the lessons of frailty and dependence "in the days of his flesh." The striking passage, 5:7-10, which we looked at in the last chapter, sets forth in graphic realism the *need* of the human Son to have the Father hear Him as He cried out in agony in the Garden.

The word translated "deal gently" in verse 2 is an interesting one. Literally it signifies "deal moderately." The setting is the high priest in relation to the age-old problem of human sin. On the one hand, since the priest stands in the presence of the Holy One, he must have a heightened awareness of the gravity of sin, of its opposition to the divine nature. Yet he should also remember humanity's weakness. That can result only as he himself senses his own frailties. Aware of his own need, he may "deal moderately" with sinners as they come to him to mediate forgiveness. The various translations have endeavored to bring out the idea: "have compassion" (KJV), "bear patiently" (NEB), "deal sympathetically" (Phillips), and "can sympathise" (Jerusalem Bible).

Let us be quite sure of one matter. While the apostle seeks to highlight the *sympathetic* high priesthood of Jesus here, he carefully avoids pressing the comparison with the Aaronites at the point of human weakness. He has told of the need of the Old Testament high priests to offer sacrifice for their own sins, but no such problem exists with Christ. His sympathy arises rather out of His own *experience* of "learning obedience" and being perfected through suffering.

Indeed, 7:27, 28 specifically denies that Jesus would ever

80

have any reason to sacrifice on His own behalf: "He has no need, like those high priests, to offer sacrifices daily, first for his own sins and then for those of the people; he did this once for all when he offered up himself. Indeed, the law appoints men in their weakness as high priests, but the word of the oath, which came later than the law, appoints a Son who has been made perfect for ever." We note here the contrast between "men in their weakness" and "a Son who has been made perfect for ever"—a direct summary of the argument of 5:1-10.

Now we come to the second way in which Christ as high priest breaks the Aaronite pattern of 5:1-4. Let us look carefully at the reasoning of 5:5, 6. As we study the passage, its logic seems curiously distorted. In verse 4 the apostle has remarked that the priesthood is not self-conferred. So also with Christ. The Father appointed Him, as the apostle attempts to show, starting with verse 5. We would *expect* him to say, "So also Christ did not exalt himself to be made a high priest, but was appointed by him who said to him, 'Thou art a priest for ever, after the order of Melchizedek.' " *Instead,* we find, "So also Christ, . . . who said to him,

'Thou art my Son,
Today I have begotten Thee';
as he says also in another place,
'Thou art a priest for ever
after the order of Melchizedek.' "

What sort of reasoning is this? Clearly, the apostle sees divine Sonship (Psalm 2:7) to be as vital to Christ's priesthood as the declaration of Psalm 110:4. Indeed, the order of citing the passages indicates that the fact of Sonship is logically prior to the appointment as priest. That is, it is because Christ is *Son* that He may be designated Melchizedekian priest.

So now we see the correlation with the argument of 2:17, 18. There we noticed that Jesus *became* qualified to be high priest by becoming man. Here, the declaration of Sonship—a status, as we saw in chapter 2, which was His before the Incarnation—enables the word of appointment. This is exactly what 7:28 says: "the word of the oath" [that is, of Psalm 110:4—"The Lord has sworn and will not change his mind . . ."]. . . appoints a Son [One who *is* Son, not *became* Son] who has been made perfect for ever [that is, by His human experiences of suffering, dependence, testing, and death]."

Thus, the second point of distinction between the Aaronite priests and Christ is in the status of each. The Old Testament high priests were taken "from among men" (5:1), but Christ is the Son who has been incarnated and so *became* qualified to be high priest.

A radically new concept of the priesthood of Jesus emerges. We see that the genuine Mediator between God and man must without equivocation truly be able to claim both as His own. He must be *both* God and man, without confusion, without dilution. And indeed it is the case with our Lord. As Son, He embraces deity, as Son "perfected," He grasps suffering, tempted, dependent humanity.

So there can ever be only one true High Priest. Only one Being in the universe can lay claim to both God and man in His own person. All the Old Testament priests but foreshadowed the Son, who would take our nature and our experiences to Himself and so be eternally qualified to mediate on our behalf.[6]

Of the seven characteristics noted in 5:1-4, then, the apostle directly applies two to Christ in 5:5-10 and denies two. The remaining three—the representative function, the cultic activity, and the atoning service—we find predicated of Him elsewhere.[7] We may summarize our discussion of Christ and Aaron as follows:

Aaron	*Christ*
Human origin	The Son "perfected"
Divine appointment	Divine appointment
Representative service	Representative service
Cultic service	Cultic service
Atoning service	Atoning service
Sympathetic service	Sympathetic service
Sin-weakened service	Sinless service

The apostle, in the passage we have been considering, argued for the divine appointment of Christ as high priest by reference to the order of Melchizedek. He returns to the same idea in a sustained argument in 6:19-7:28.

Christ and Melchizedek

The figure of Melchizedek has aroused speculation for more than two thousand years. The rabbis puzzled over the scanty references to his person, early Christians found themselves fascinated by his relation to Christ, modern Christians debate the cryptic account of him in Hebrews.

Such interest is all the more remarkable when we consider that only five verses out of the entire Old Testament mention him—Genesis 14:17-20 and Psalm 110:4. Suddenly, without explanation, the person of Melchizedek appears amid the stories of the patriarchs. A contemporary of Abraham, Melchizedek *blesses* him. He is a priest long before the Lord proclaims the Jewish order of priesthood to Moses at Sinai. And long after the establishment of that priesthood, the voice of the psalmist heralds the rise of a new priest, one whose line will link with Melchizedek, not Aaron.

Melchizedek, in fact, was an embarrassment to some of the rabbis. In an attempt to establish him firmly in the line of Israel, some identified him with the patriarch Shem (the genealogies permit it). Another ingenious solution held that, because Melchizedek blessed Abraham before blessing God (see Genesis 14:17-20), the priesthood was taken from him and given to Abraham.

If they had only the Old Testament references to Melchizedek, Christians probably would not have shown much interest in him. But he figures prominently in the New Testament. All the references, however, occur in one book—Hebrews. And here, in chapter 7 we find perhaps the most puzzling words of the entire New Testament: "He is without father or mother or genealogy, and has neither beginning of days nor end of life, but resembling the Son of God he continues a priest for ever" (7:3).

What sort of a being is he? A man from another planet? Christ coming down to earth in human form nearly two thousand years before Bethlehem? Or, as some Adventists have maintained—and there even exists an apocryphal statement attributed to Ellen G. White to the effect—that he is the Holy Spirit? No wonder the passing of the centuries has not diminished interest in the conundrum of Melchizedek.

Let us lay aside the puzzle of 7:3 for a moment. Presently we shall trace the argumentation of Hebrews 7 and show just how Melchizedek enters into the theology of priesthood that the apostle is developing. But at the outset we must be clear on two matters.

First, *we completely miss the point of Hebrews if we focus our attention on Melchizedek instead of Christ.* The summary statement concerning Melchizedek of 7:1-3 ends with the assertion, *"resembling the Son of God* he continues a priest for ever."* The priest-king of ancient Salem is chronologically prior to the incarnate Son, but theologically the Son is prior. Only on this basis can we account for the reasoning that would have otherwise been, as might be expected, "and the Son of God resembles *his* priesthood." Thus, only by considering the figure of Melchizedek in a subsidiary relationship to the priesthood of Christ can we rightly discern the apostle's intent.

A quick overview of the entire seventh chapter confirms our finding. We may break down the flow of thought into the following paragraphs:

Verses 1-3: A description of Melchizedek, who is likened to the Son of God.

Verses 4-10: Melchizedek shown to be greater than Levi, since Abraham paid tithe to and was blessed by him.

Verses 11-14: The prediction of a change in the law of the Levitical priesthood.

Verses 15-19: The new priesthood of Christ based on indestructible life and bringing full access to God.

Verses 20-22: The new priesthood confirmed by an oath.

Verses 23-25: The new priesthood confined to only one priest, Jesus Christ.

Verses 26-28: The new priesthood has a sinless Son as priest.

The cryptic third verse and the convoluted reasoning of the chapter have led students of Hebrews to an undue concern with Melchizedek. But no more than Abraham or Levi is Melchizedek the center of the apostle's interest. In fact, the apostle does not mention him after verse 17.

Second, *we fail to understand the role of Melchizedek in the argument until we see the importance of Psalm 110:4 for the apostle.* Specifically, he does not launch upon an exposition of the Melchizedek passage of Genesis 14:17-20 and thereby move to an application to Christ. Rather, the prediction of a Messianic priesthood "after the order of Melchizedek" found in Psalm 110:4 leads him *back* to the Genesis account—the only other mention of Melchizedek in the Old Testament.

It is instructive to see the way in which he plays on Psalm 110:4 in the course of the sermon. The passage comes up over and over and is undoubtedly of key importance. He quotes it in full or in part, each time using it to give Scriptural backing to the particular point he happens to be making:

1. 5:6: Quoted in full; the totality of the divine utterance indicates the divine *appointment* of the perfected Son to the high-priestly office (5:10).

2. 6:20: The last part only—"priest for ever after the order of Melchizedek"—quoted. The reference introduces the summary of Genesis 14:17-20 in 7:1-3 and forms the basis for the entire discussion of Jesus as Melchizedekian high priest, which fills chapter 7.

3. 7:11: An allusion to Psalm 110:4—here the author uses the prediction of the rise of another priesthood in the psalm to argue the *necessity* of a change in the Levitical priesthood.

4. 7:15-17: Again Psalm 110:4 is cited in full. The point here is that God has set forth a *new order* of priesthood, one that does not require physical descent from the tribe of Levi.

5. 7:20, 21: Only part of the divine words are quoted: "Thou art a priest for ever." Instead, the emphasis falls on the words of the *oath* that establish Him as a priest: "The Lord has sworn and will not change his mind."

6. 7:24: An allusion only, picking up the words of Psalm

110:4, which indicate Christ's *continuing* priesthood: a priest *"for ever."*

7. 7:28: A final allusion to Psalm 110:4, gathering together the ideas of divine appointment, divine oath, and eternal priesthood.

We may show the subtle shifts of emphasis in the use of Psalm 110:4 by underlining the key words in each of the above occurrences:

1. 5:6: "a *priest* for ever"
2. 6:20: "the order of *Melchizedek*"
3. 7:11: "the *order* of Melchizedek"
4. 7:15-17: "the *order of Melchizedek*"
5. 7:20, 21: "the *Lord has sworn*"
6. 7:24: *"for ever"*
7. 7:28 (NEB)—"priest appointed by the words of the oath . . . is the Son . . . for ever."

With these two insights we may now outline the argument of Hebrews 7. In keeping with the purposes of this book, we cannot produce a thoroughgoing exegesis. Our purpose, rather, is to guide the interested reader along the flow of the apostle's thought.

Verses 1-3: Melchizedek likened to the Son of God. We note the apostle's selectivity of detail here. Although he mentions Melchizedek as king of Salem, he does not develop the royal aspect. It is in keeping with his concern throughout Hebrews, where he merely refers to the regnant Son (1:4, 13; 8:1; 10:12) but says no more. His consuming interest centers in the priesthood of the Son, and hence of Melchizedek. The latter provides a convenient point of departure, since his sacerdotal office is both non-Levitical and (as shown in the next paragraph of chapter 7) greater than the Levitical.

Even in dealing with Melchizedek as priest, however, the apostle remains selective. He makes no allusion to the bread and wine brought out by Melchizedek,[8] not attempting the obvious Eucharistic application.[9]

What points does he then wish to draw from the sacerdotal office of Melchizedek? Three, apparently: the greatness of his office (verses 1, 2), his lack of genealogy (verse 3), and the continuing character of his office (verse 3). The first point he elaborates in verses 4-10, the second in verses 11-19, and the third in verses 20-25.

We come now to the curious words of verse 3—"without father or mother or genealogy, and has neither beginning of days nor end of life." Do they predicate a supernatural, other-worldly character of Melchizedek? Most assuredly not. Nothing in the Genesis account suggests that he was anything but another human being. But note—neither do we find any record of his parentage, birth, or death there. He comes abruptly onto the stage, stars in one brief scene, and then disappears forever. It is this total view of Melchizedek from which the apostle argues in Hebrews 7:3—that view with its omissions as well as its data. That is, the *Genesis record* of Melchizedek, rather than the man himself, furnishes the foundation of the apostle's reasoning.[10]

As in so many other instances, the archaeologist's spade has uncovered remains that shed light on the problem. In an ancient inscription Abdu-Heba, a king of Jerusalem in the 14th century BC, writes to the Egyptian Pharaoh: "Behold this land of Jerusalem. (It was) not my father (and) not my mother (who) gave (it) to me, (but) the arm of the mighty king (which) gave (it) to me."[11]

That is, the ancients considered the founder of a dynasty to be without father or mother, without genealogy. Here we possibly have the explanation of the Melchizedek description of 7:3.

Verses 4-10: Melchizedek greater than Levi. The punch line comes in verses 9 and 10. Although Abraham has been to the fore throughout verses 4-8, the apostle really wants to get to Levi—and so to the priesthood named for him. His reasoning is:
1. Melchizedek greater than Abraham because:
    a. He received Abraham's tithes.
    b. He blessed Abraham.
2. Melchizedek greater than Levi because:
    a. Levi (through Abraham) paid tithes to him.
    b. "He lives" (verse 8), i.e., *in the record* he continues a priest for ever.

The logic may strike our minds as forced and artificial. With our emphasis on the individual, we find it difficult to accept the idea of the unborn Levi paying tithes through his ancestor Abraham. A great truth surfaces here, however—that of corporate personality. The Bible would remind us that, modern emphases to the contrary, invisible cords bind our individuality to other members of the human race.

The point that emerges from the paragraph is clear: Melchizedek, who is a non-Levite (see verse 6) is greater than Levi. The unstated conclusion is therefore that the Melchizedekian priesthood is greater than the Levitical.

Verses 11-14: prediction of a change from the Levitical priesthood. The argument centers in Psalm 110:4. That psalm, by its prediction of the rise of a new priest—one after the order of Melchizedek—points up the *inadequacy* of the old sacerdotal system. Here the apostle introduces a term—"perfection"—that will reoccur frequently in the following chapters as he deals with the priestly work of Christ. His putting of the matter in verse 11—"if perfection had been attainable through the Levitical priesthood . . ."—shows that it was *not*. The apostle's argument proceeds as follows:

1. The prediction of a new priesthood shows the inadequacy of the old priesthood.

2. The rise of a Melchizedekian priest entails a change in the law of priesthood.

3. Thus Jesus came from Judah, a nonsacerdotal tribe, but is priest under the new order.

We should avoid confusion as to the use of "law" here. The context makes it clear that the apostle means the law of priesthood—specifically, the Old Testament requirement that limited the sacerdotal office to the descendants of Levi.

Verses 15-19: rise of the new priesthood. He elaborates the ideas of the previous paragraph in terms of Christ, High Priest of the new order. That is:

1. Christ is not priest by birth but by
   a. the divine word (Psalm 110:4);
   b. "the . . . indestructible life."

2. So the new priesthood supersedes the old Levitical priesthood.

Once again the apostle brings in the idea of "perfection"—"the law [i.e., the law of Levitical office] made nothing perfect." Verse 19, by contrast, gives us a clue to his meaning: through the new order we *draw near* to God. We shall notice in the next chapter how he enlarges upon this matter as he discusses the sacrifice of Christ in terms of "perfection."

Verses 20-22: Priesthood confirmed by an oath. Another argument for the superiority of Christ's high priesthood surfaces here. Unlike the Levitical priests, Jesus was appointed to the sacred office by the word of divine oath.

Verses 23-25: The new priesthood unchangeable. The apostle raises a further point of superiority. Whereas the old priesthood necessarily entailed a succession of priests, Christ's office is permanent because of His eternal life. Continuity of person ensures perpetual availability of salvation and strengthens Christian confidence.

Verses 26-28: The new high priest is a sinless Son. The final, climactic word now falls. "We . . . have *such* a high priest," says the apostle, "holy, blameless, unstained, separated from sinners, exalted above the heavens." He needs no offering in His own behalf, for He is the Son!

As we look back over chapter 7, we see that the overriding concern is in the *superiority* of Jesus as high priest. In at least eight ways He is greater than the Levitical priests:

—because Melchizedek was greater than Abraham, as shown by the blessing and receipt of tithe (4-10);
—because the prediction of the new priesthood indicates the inadequacy of the old (11);
—because by Him comes "perfection" (11, 19);
—because His priesthood is founded on "indestructible life," not genealogy (15, 16, 24);
—because it was made by a divine oath (20-22);
—because He is one instead of many (23);
—because of His sinless character (26, 27);
—because He is Son (28).

Our study has illumined the manner in which the Melchizedek discussion advances the argument of Hebrews. As the comparison with Moses showed Christ as faithful high priest and the Aaron passage highlighted His merciful, sympathetic person, so the comparison with Melchizedek was helpful in several ways: (1) it pointed to the *eternal* high-priesthood of Christ; (2) it demonstrated the *superiority* of His priesthood over the Levitical system; and (3) it explained how Jesus, who did not qualify by descent to be a priest according to the old system, could rightly be set out in sacerdotal terms.

Another likely reason for the apostle's dealing with Melchizedek will emerge as we turn to the matter of the place of Jesus' priestly work.

The Place of Christ's Priesthood

We have increasing evidence of considerable Jewish speculation concerning a heavenly sanctuary and liturgy both before and at the time of the writing of Hebrews. Thought seems to have run along two main lines—a realistic conception and an allegorizing view.

In the Testament of Levi, we read, "And in it [the heavenly Tabernacle] are the archangels, who minister and make propitiation to the Lord for all the sins of ignorance of the righteous; offering to the Lord a sweet-smelling savor, a reasonable and bloodless offering."[12]
Similarly, in the book of Jubilees: "And may the Lord give to thee . . . to serve in His sanctuary as the angels of the presence and the holy ones."[13]

The Testament of Dan calls for man to "draw near unto God and unto the angel that intercedeth for you, for he is a mediator between God and man."[14]

In each pseudepigraphical book (dating from the first or second centuries before Jesus) we find a realistic conception of a heavenly sanctuary. Likewise, we notice beliefs in angelic ministry and mediatorial work within that tabernacle. The Dead Sea Scrolls present a similar picture.

In contrast to the view of an actual heavenly sanctuary and liturgy stands the allegorizing position. Philo Judaeus, a Jewish scholar of the first century AD, wrote of the heavenly sanctuary, "The highest, and in the truest sense the holy temple of God is, as we must believe, the whole universe, having for its sanctuary the most sacred part of all existence, even heaven, for its votive ornaments of the stars, for its priests the angels who are servitors to His powers, unbodied souls, not compounds of rational and irrational nature." [15] For Philo, the high priest of the Temple at Jerusalem symbolized the divine *Logos* (word) in the cosmos. [16]

The preceding statements help provide us with a background in sanctuary thought contemporary with the writing of Hebrews. Obviously, while the ideas of heavenly temple and liturgy may fall strangely on modern ears, they were not at all uncommon in the first century. Now we may better understand why the apostle could basically *assume* the ideas of priesthood and sanctuary. He does not set out to prove such ideas, but rather to show the place of Christ *within* their framework.

But what was his own conception of the heavenly sanctuary and liturgy? He says little about them, writing of "the sanctuary and the true tent which is set up not by man but the Lord" (8:2). The apostle tells us that the sanctuary made by Moses was but "a copy and shadow of the heavenly sanctuary" (8:5). That celestial tabernacle is "the greater and more perfect tent (not made with hands, that is, not of this creation)" (9:11).

While he does not enter upon a description of the heavenly sanctuary and liturgy, his language suggests several important conclusions. First, he holds to their *reality*. His concern throughout the sermon is to ground Christian confidence in objective *facts*, as we have seen. *Real* deity, *real* humanity, *real* priesthood—and we may add, a *real* ministry in a *real* sanctuary. Second, it is the heavenly and not the earthly that is the genuine. The earthly was but a pale shadow, a temporary device pointing to the real. (This point, by the way, is important in interpretation: The real will explain the shadow, and not vice versa.) Third, his basic conception of the heavenly sanctuary does not fit the allegorizing pattern of Philo. True, the apostle uses some of

Philo's terminology in his brief description of the heavenly sanctuary. His emphasis on *time,* however—Christ's *becoming* a high priest—seems to break the Philonian model.

Now we can better grasp the course of the argument regarding Christ as High Priest. Against contemporary ideas of angelic ministry, even mediatorial work, in a heavenly sanctuary, the apostle affirms the vast superiority of the Son. *He alone is our High Priest!* Angels have a role to play in the divine purpose, but we must never place them alongside the eternally one High Priest.

Likewise with Melchizedek. A scroll discovered in Cave No. 4 at Qumran has a fair amount to say about him. The scroll is in a bad state of preservation, but it seems clear that the Dead Sea sectaries associated Melchizedek with priestly activity in the heavenly sanctuary. The Book of Hebrews rules out any such ideas, which may have caused doubt among the author's own Christian hearers. The apostle asserts the uniqueness of Jesus, not of Melchizedek. The latter is but a curious figure out of the Old Testament, the record of whom forms a helpful point of departure to argue for the superlative qualities of the one, eternal, heavenly High Priest.

The Time of Christ's Priesthood

We may close our discussion of Christ as priest by raising one last set of questions: When did He become our high priest? Was He eternally priest? Will He remain forever our high priest?

To the first two, Hebrews has a clear-cut answer. No, He was not eternally a priest, but He *became* a priest. Two main arguments reveal the apostle's intent.

The first relates to Christ's *qualifications* for priesthood. We have noticed them carefully in the present and previous chapters. The apostle argued that the Incarnation was *necessary* for Him to become a high priest. By taking our nature and by sharing our experiences of test, suffering, and need, the Son was "perfected." As both God and man, He was ready in His person for the divine appointment. Since we have examined them already, we need not pursue them any further in our present discussion.

There is a second argument. At 2:17 we read, ''Therefore he had to be made like his brethren in every respect, so that he might become a merciful and faithful high priest in the service of God, to make expiation for the sins of the people.'' The last part—the making expiation for sins—receives elaboration in 9:1 to 10:18 and will occupy our attention in the forthcoming chapter. At 8:3, however, the apostle declares, ''For every high priest is appointed to offer gifts and sacrifices; *hence it is necessary for this priest also to have something to offer.*'' That is, as the Incarnation prepared His person for priesthood, so it also provided His priestly sacrifice—of Himself.

On the basis of these clear-cut arguments of Hebrews we hold that Christ (according to Hebrews) did not have an eternal sacerdotal office. Strictly speaking, we may not speak of Him as priest until after the Resurrection. Not uncommonly we term the petition in the Garden (John 17) as the high-priestly prayer of Christ. But that goes against the theology of Hebrews.

What then—one may counter—of people in Old Testament times? Did they have no heavenly priest? Since the apostle is silent on the question, we are not at liberty to pursue it. Our work in the succeeding chapter may provide some pointers, but no more. (We will see, for instance, how the Old Testament services were but symbols imposed until the reality that was Calvary came once for all upon mankind.)

It leaves us with the third question we raised above. Will Christ *remain* a priest forever, as the psalm designates?

Here also the apostle has no direct answer for us. His reasoning in terms of Christ's perpetual priesthood (7:23-25, especially) does not address the issue. Rather, it shows the *contrast* between the many successive Levitical priests and our One Priest for all time.

Going outside Hebrews, we might argue for an eventual cessation of Christ's priesthood. When the agelong sin problem has been finally resolved, and sin and sinners no longer exist—when, in the language of the Apocalypse, we find no more Temple in the New Jerusalem, ''for its temple is the Lord God the

Almighty and the Lamb'' (Revelation 21:22)—will not Christ's sacerdotal work have ceased?

Yet, if we have read aright the apostle's theology relative to Christ as high priest, we may see an eternal, never-ending sense to the "for ever" of Psalm 110:4. Christ *became* high priest. What He became, He is—forever is. He is eternally the perfected Son. His human experiences will always be part of Him. *Becoming* Priest, He must remain Priest—forever.

And so with His sacrifice also. Will it not be by virtue of it that the people of God will eternally live? Who would suggest that, ages hence, we shall have outgrown its saving power? He *died* in time, an irreversible, eternal fact. The Eternal Priest is Sacrifice—forever.

The Priest: Basis for Absolute Confidence

In the light of our discussion so far we can better appreciate the richness of the conception of Jesus as our High Priest. At first sight the concept seems distant from our situation and problems, yet it is pregnant with spiritual meaning for Christians today.

Its primary thrust is to place our religion squarely on an objective basis. While Christianity at heart is a living relationship with a living God, so that God's followers may have something worth saying when they talk of "Christian experience," the appeal to personal "knowledge" is a hazardous one. Who knows whether our so-called "experience" but echoes our own consciousness, as Feuerbach claimed a century ago?[17] Today when psychology has laid bare the inner recesses of being and has (seemingly) come up with naturalistic explanations for all facets of our emotions and behavior, can we press the traditional appeal to personal knowledge of Christ?

And further, our feelings are so unreliable, so changeable, that we cannot place weight upon them. That we *feel* close to God does not verify the idea. That we *feel* far from Him does not show it to be the case.

The Book of Hebrews, with its preeminent concept of Jesus as Heavenly High Priest, shifts the ground of Christian living. The basis of Christian confidence, argues the apostle, does not lie in our subjective states. It is not vulnerable to the empirical observations and rationalizations of psychologists. Nor is it a matter of doubt, of the haunting fear that our God-talk is but the reflection of our own mental processes. No—it lies *outside* ourselves. Jesus as High Priest is a fixed, immovable datum. No matter what we may *feel* or opponents of our religion may assert, He remains High Priest in heaven for us.

Because it is the perfected *Son* whom the Father appointed as our High Priest, we may rest assured that God is on our side. He understands the heat of our trials, feels within Himself how weak we are, sympathizes with our struggles. The Exalted One is the All-Merciful One.

And not merely merciful. Since He overcame in the conflicts of human life, He ever lives to provide timely help. The throne of God is the throne of grace. No matter what the hour, no matter how isolated—or busy—the place, the cry of the petitioner meets with instant and effective response from the heavenly Temple.

He is both *faithful* and *abiding* as our High Priest, argues the apostle. In that constancy of character and life rests our hope, our assurance. He is no pagan deity who may frown at us at any moment. We need ring no temple bell to summon Him from sleep or let Him know we desire His attention. Because He is faithful forever as our High Priest, He is able to save for all time those who come to God through Him.

Alone, all alone—this is the chilling realization of so many modern thinkers as they contemplate the vastnesses of space and the enigma of human existence. Like Coleridge's ancient mariner, they feel cut off from any port of meaning or destiny, strange creatures of sense and thought in a dark, cold, forbidding universe.

But Hebrews tells us that we are not alone. We have a High Priest who shares our nature as He shared our human lot.

One final thought presses itself upon us as we contemplate the wealth of meaning in the conception of Jesus as our Heavenly High Priest. The apostle's reasoning has made it evident that He *alone* qualifies for this designation. He stands unique, apart from all others, be they so-called priests of the Old Testament or of the non-Christian religions. True, man in his sense of alienation from the Source of all being has sought out mediators, has set apart religious functionaries who by one means or other have tried to stand in the gap between God and man, to represent man before the presence of Deity. But all such figures, despite what they may have claimed or been called, were not priests. Only the One Being in the entire universe could rightly own that term. He who in His own person brings together both deity and humanity is the one, single, only High Priest in truth.

So the church must preserve in her theology the uniqueness of the sacerdotalism of our Lord. No man by ordination may claim mediatorial office, no minister of the gospel is to encourage priestly veneration. The people of God must constantly direct their attention to the One who ministers on our behalf in the heavenly temple.

There, and there alone, lies the ground of our faith. In His *person,* in His human *experiences,* in His *faithfulness,* in His *sympathy,* in His *constancy,* we find absolute confidence for Christian life in our time.

Our studies in this chapter have already revealed how the Book of Hebrews sets Jesus forth in both person and *deed.* That is, He is at once High Priest and Sacrifice. We turn now to the second idea as we study the fourth basis for Christian assurance in the sermon to the Hebrews.

---

[1] For instance, the massive sacrifices at the dedication of the first Temple (2 Chronicles 5:6; 7:5). Moffatt's comment is perceptive: "The business of a priest was often that of a butcher; blood flowed, blood was splashed about" (*The Epistle to the Hebrews,* xlvi).

[2] Hebrews 3:16; 7:14; 8:5; 9:19; 10:28; 11:23, 24; 12:21.

[3] Cf John 20:21: "As the Father has sent me, even so I send you."

[4] See article "Hasmoneans," *Interpreter's Dictionary of the Bible,* Vol. 2, pp. 529-535.

[5] Note especially the self-serving counsel of Caiaphas in John 11:49-52.

[6] We see also the misunderstanding of Christ's person involved in any post New Testament claim for men to be Christian priests.

[7] See Hebrews 2:17, 18; 4:14-16; 7:25; 8:3; and especially 9:1 to 10:18.

[8] The Midrash regards the bread and wine as symbols of the showbread and

drink-offering, or the Torah itself (*Beresh. R.* 43. 18). Philo allegorizes the wine as the "divine intoxication" that raises the soul to lofty thoughts of God (*Legum Allegoria,* 3. 25, 26).

[9] Is the omission deliberate? At the least we may conclude that the apostle has no sacramental interest in his sermon. Efforts by expositors of Hebrews to see allusions to the Mass or sacraments in the document meet a serious obstacle in this passage.

[10] Compare Uriah Smith's editorial in *Review and Herald,* Nov. 5, 1895: "Lastly, let it further be borne in mind that the expressions, which are to many so perplexing, are written from the standpoint of the record we have of Melchizedek, which give us no particulars on these points. These expressions are: 'without father,' 'without mother,' 'having neither beginning of days, nor end of life,' 'of whom it is witnessed, that he liveth.' The record tells us nothing about his pedigree, his birth, or death. So far as the record goes, no beginning nor end of life is given; and it was the custom, therefore, among the Jews, to speak of such as having no genealogy, no mother, no father, no beginning of days, nor end of life. And considering that all these expressions are used simply from the standpoint of the *record,* there is no difficulty. Melchisedek suddenly appears upon the scene of action, an eminent servant of God, combining, in his own person the double office of king and priest. All before him is blank; all following him is blank. Neither birth nor death appearing in the scene, he becomes a fitting prototype of Christ in his position of priest-king in this dispensation."

[11] James Pritchard, *Ancient Near Eastern Texts* (Princeton: Princeton University Press, 1969), p. 488.

[12] *Testament of Levi* 3:5, 6.

[13] *Jubilees* 31:14.

[14] *Testament of Dan* 6:2.

[15] *De specialibus legibus,* I, 12:66, Loeb Classical Library, (Philo), Vol. VII, pp. 137, 138.

[16] *Quaestiones et solutiones in Exodum,* Loeb Classical Library, Supplement II (Cambridge: Harvard University, 1953), p. 48.

[17] Ludwig Feuerbach, *Lectures on the Essence of Religion* (New York: Harper & Row, 1967, first published in 1851), p. 17.

Chapter 5

The Sacrifice— Once for All

"Yet here's a spot. . . .
Out, damned spot! out, I say! . . .
What, will these hands ne'er be clean? . . .
Here's the smell of the blood still. All the
perfumes of Arabia will not sweeten this little hand."[1]

Lady Macbeth walks the stairs in tormented sleep. As she descends, making washing motions with her hands, the burden of murder—by her and her husband—lies heavy on her conscience.

Shakespeare, in this graphic scene, has penned a portrait of us all. We are all troubled by deep-seated feelings of unease, of being out of touch with the fundamental order of the cosmos, of falling short of its ideal, and of being in a measure personally *responsible*.

Man is the great dreamer of creation. Surrounded by a world of imperfection, he nevertheless imagines the perfect. Conditioned on all sides, he visualizes the unconditioned. In a natural order where time and chance happen to all, where the weak go down and the strong survive, in a social order where—so it seems—every man has his price, he realizes his own moral failure. In Bouquet's phrase, he suffers "numinous uneasiness,"[2] a gut sense of fundamental violation of the order of his being.

It is out of numinous uneasiness that religions have arisen. By one way or another the world's faiths endeavor to bring peace to mankind's troubled conscience. In Biblical parlance they offer a solution to the "sin" problem. In some cases the way offered is extremely demanding, calling for hardship, loss of home and worldly goods, requiring pilgrimage, celibacy, isolation. But often so painful is the troubled conscience that such harsh measures—even the ultimate test of forfeiting life itself—find devotees.

We have seen how Hebrews portrays Jesus Christ in the role of High Priest. But what He *is* is not enough. Can He provide a remedy to the age-old, universal "sin" sickness? That is, beyond what He *is,* what has He *done* to still the numinous unease of mankind? Unless we receive a satisfying answer, our talk of assurance and confidence will be whistling in the dark.

So we have come to the ultimate question. And to it the apostle sets forth the ultimate reply. His long, involved theological argument has been preparing for this moment of truth. As the first seven chapters—with homiletical asides—worked out the high priesthood of Jesus, so the remainder of the theology, ending with 10:18, will present in thoroughgoing fashion the accomplishment of Jesus, that past deed which gives Him, as High Priest, "something to offer" (8:3).

The reasoning is compact and detailed. But it is well worth the effort expended in wrestling to unlock its progress. He who succeeds in following the apostle's presentation, especially in 9:1–10:18, will understand why the ancient document rings with such vibrant confidence.

Our efforts to understand Jesus as Sacrifice will center in the text of Hebrews 8-10. Rather than following its order rigidly, however, we will seek clarity by a topical analysis. The following aspects of the argument will lay bare the root of the presentation:

The Human Predicament

The Old Testament Services

The Role of Blood
The Accomplishment of Calvary
Once for All
We shall take them up in turn.

The Human Predicament

In the proem, a handful of words sums up the entire course of the Son's earthly career: "when he had made purification for sins." The birth, the preaching, the miracles—His supreme accomplishment sets them all aside. Clearly, in the apostle's thinking, the Incarnation had one superlative purpose—to deal with the sin problem of mankind.

But let us take another look at his words. He gives us here a vital clue to what will follow, as he states that Christ made *purification* for sins. Rarely have the commentaries mentioned this clue. Writer after writer passes over it and begins to talk of "forgiveness" or "redemption."

Purification, however, is *not* forgiveness or redemption. Accustomed to lumping together the various New Testament ways of describing the work of Christ, we fail to hear what the authors were saying. Forgiveness comes out of a debt context—it is literally the cancellation of a debt. We see this meaning preserved in Matthew's form of the Lord's Prayer: "Forgive us our debts as we forgive our debtors."[3] Redemption, on the other hand, is a marketplace metaphor. To redeem something is literally to buy it back, e.g., from the pawnbroker's store. Besides forgiveness and redemption, one finds many other New Testament metaphors or models of the work of Christ,[4] but the one Hebrews employs here is that of purification. It is a *cleanliness* model. Christ's work is to wash away the dirt or defilement that burdens our conscience.

Does the language of defilement and purification reappear in chapters 8-10? Most certainly:

9:13, 14: "For if the sprinkling of defiled persons with the blood of goats and bulls and with the ashes of a heifer sanctifies for the purification of the flesh, how much more shall the blood of Christ, who through the eternal Spirit offered himself without blemish to God, purify your conscience from dead works to serve the living God."

9:22: "Indeed, under the law almost everything is purified with blood, and without the shedding of blood there is no forgiveness of sins."

9:23: "Thus it was necessary for the copies of the heavenly things to be purified with these rites, but the heavenly things themselves with better sacrifices than these."

10:1, 2: "For since the law has but a shadow of the good things to come instead of the true form of these realities, it can never, by the same sacrifices which are continually offered year after year, make perfect those who draw near. Otherwise, would they not have ceased to be offered? If the worshipers had once been cleansed, they would no longer have any consciousness of sin."

10:22: "Let us draw near with a true heart in full assurance of faith, with our hearts sprinkled clean from an evil conscience and our bodies washed with pure water."

Not merely incidental references, they point to the very heart of the argumentation. The first (9:13, 14) contrasts the old Sanctuary services with the new, but in terms of purification, the key idea being *"how much more."* The old cultus purifies the flesh, but the new the conscience. The second (9:22) links blood and purification in a key text that we must examine carefully later. The third (9:23) is a startling verse. It argues that the state of earthly things (i.e., the earthly sanctuary) is such that it requires purification, and that the "heavenly things" (the celestial tabernacle) *also* require cleansing—but with better sacrifices. At 10:1, 2 we hear an echo of 9:13, 14—the failure of the old cultus to bring thoroughgoing purification. In 10:22, however, decisive cleansing has been obtained—through the blood of Christ.

A common idea runs throughout the passage. Man's basic problem is that he is dirty, defiled. Indeed, the *universal* need is for purgation. If Christ is to solve the cosmic predicament, He must be able to purify. We shall not grasp the logic of the presentation until we give full weight to this point.

Three other allusions to defilement appear in Hebrews. Each occurs outside chapters 8-10 and is unstudied in nature. In 7:26 the apostle describes Christ as an "unstained" High Priest. At 12:15 he warns against the "root of bitterness" that may spring up to defile many. He exhorts at 13:4 that "the marriage bed be [kept] undefiled." The scattered references are significant. They indicate that the language of defilement and purification is not something that the apostle temporarily employs, to be set aside as we discern his deeper meaning.

The apostle's emphasis on defilement and purification is worth reflection. It is not a curiosity in the history of ideas or religion—far from it. Indeed, as we study into religion, we find that both ideas are universal and timeless. Paul Ricoeur, in *The Symbolism of Evil*,[5] has shown that they enshrine the most basic awareness of the language of confession—before feelings of guilt arise, man realizes he is dirty, religiously defiled. We see this awareness in the "negative confession" of ancient Egypt—"I have not defiled myself in the pure places of the god of my city"[6]—as in the modern book of *Revelations in Tenrikyo:* "When you have swept dust cleanly, I will certainly bring you a miraculous salvation."[7] Also we observe it in the supposed power of the Ganges and the other sacred rivers of India to purge away sin, and in Japanese rituals of sprinkling salt and bathing to ward off defilement.

Scholars have made extensive studies of the phenomena of defilement and purification. An entire international congress of the history of religions revolved around the topic.[8] We cannot enter into a detailed study of the subject here. Suffice it to notice that the data of defilement point to a symbology of evil that has been of fundamental and enduring significance in the life of mankind, irrespective of culture. It suggests a quasi-material, quasi-moral evil power that is readily transmissible. Defilement represents the disruptive element, the force of disorder and chaos that stands over against the individual's existence, his society, and finally the cosmos. Thus, the defiled person is both in danger himself and a source of peril to ordered relationships.

May I suggest that this most basic sense of our fundamental

religious uneasiness still lies close to modern man? True, we have no holy rivers in the U.S.A., nor do we seek cleansing by sprinkling the ashes of a sacrificed heifer (as did the Israelites of old) or by passing through a tunnel of smoke (as do primitive tribes). But the *ideas* of defilement and purification exist deep in our subconscious and emerge in language. Why do we talk of "dirty tricks" and "filthy stories"? Why do people develop neuroses about germs and dust, as did Howard Hughes? And, even for "normal" people, why the great American passion for cleanliness—shown by the outpouring on detergents, deodorants, washing machines, and bathrooms? Perhaps the old adage about cleanliness and godliness touched a religious nerve deep in the subconscious.

So the apostle's account of the human predicament bears careful study. While it is not the traditional model of the lawcourt, with "guilt" and "justification" the principal terms, it is nonetheless significant. It brings out an insight that has remained half hidden in the West for many years. We turn now to see how well the Old Testament Sanctuary services coped with man's problem of defilement.

The Old Testament Services

We must exercise special care in dealing with the Old Testament Sanctuary and its services. On one hand, we may so dwell on the differences from the real—the work of Christ—that we reduce the old to a system of useless ceremonies. On the other, we may so underscore actual or supposed continuities with the real that we obliterate the distinctiveness of Calvary in a religious flattening-out.

Here we meet full face that matter which surfaced in our discussion of 1:1-4: how to rightly balance Old Testament with New; how to maintain the *value* of the old—for, as Hebrews takes everywhere for granted, God Himself gave it—and yet to rightly bring out the element of *newness* in the sacrifice of Christ.

Let us remind ourselves from the outset that the apostle has not embarked on a thoroughgoing treatment of the Old Testament cultus. Rather, his concern is the *old in relation to the new.* He endeavors, as we saw earlier, to confirm tired Christians in the certainty of their faith, not to present a full-blown treatise on Old Testament religion. The key word of Hebrews, we suggested, is *better,* and the idea reigns throughout chapters 8-10. Thus, in 8:6 he speaks of a better covenant and at 9:14 of the "how much more" of the blood of Christ.

Inevitably the old cultus will show up unfavorably alongside the new. The apostle does not cast scorn upon it, as some exegetes of Hebrews have concluded. He does not argue that the old is *bad.* (How could it be, when it came from God?) Rather, he emphasizes that it is *inadequate,* and—for here is the bottom line—that the work of Jesus Christ fully meets all its deficiencies.

As the apostle works his way to that conclusion, the reasoning clusters around four ideas: covenant, access, conscience, perfection. We will understand him as we come to grips with each.

The first term, "covenant," has engendered much theological discussion over the years. Many have debated whether the "old" covenant was legalistic or not, in contrast to the "new" covenant of grace. Other passages of the Bible, especially Galatians 3:15-18; 4:21-31, heavily touch upon the issue here. At times the respective arguments have been tortuous and the exchanges heated.

Let us deal with Hebrews on its own terms. If we will but follow the text itself, refraining from importing other Scriptures and theological baggage, we may grasp the argument quite readily.

The first mention of "covenant" occurs at 7:22: "This makes Jesus the surety of a better covenant." If we look back over the context, we notice that it is the divine oath constituting Jesus as Melchizedekian high priest which leads to the apostle's assertion (verses 20, 21). That is, from the first use of "covenant" he associates the idea with priesthood. Further, going back to the rise of the argument (verse 15), we see that the apostle contrasts the Levitical priesthood with that of Jesus. In other words, there exists a correlation of better priesthood with better covenant.

104

Chapter 8 confirms and elaborates the idea. Verse 6 expressly states that the ministry of Christ "is as much more excellent than the old as the covenant he mediates is better." The following verse designates the old covenant as faulty and for proof repeats the citation of Jeremiah 31:31-34. Here the reasoning parallels that of 7:11, 12. Just as the prediction of a *new* order of priesthood showed the imperfection of the old priesthood, so the prophecy of the rise of a new covenant demonstrates the faulty character of the old covenant. The new inevitably will supersede the old—the exact point of 8:13.

The quotation from Jeremiah is a long one.[9] It makes several points: the prediction of a new covenant, the failure of the people to continue in the old, the internalization of law under the new covenant, its personal religion, its teaching function, and its putting away of sins. Here indeed are the "better promises" that the writer referred to in verse 6.

Not all aspects have significance for the argument, however. Indeed, as we see how the apostle goes on to develop his ideas, only one—apart from the actual prediction of the rise of a new covenant—emerges with clarity. It is the final promise of Jeremiah 31:34—"I will remember their sins no more." His return to talk about covenant (at 9:15-18) demonstrates the conceptual importance. After speaking of the sacrifice of Christ in contrast to the death of animals, he says, "Therefore he is the mediator of a new covenant, so that those who are called may receive the promised eternal inheritance, since a death has occurred which redeems them from the transgressions under the first covenant."

Verses 10:15-18 provide further confirmation. At the close of his long discussion about the death of Christ, he quotes again the Jeremianic passage, abbreviating it to the opening and closing lines. After citing, "I will remember their sins and their misdeeds no more," he ends the theology proper of Hebrews with, "Where there is forgiveness of these, there is no longer any offering for sin."

The *cultic* implications of "covenant" will now be clear. Another passage underscores the point. Verses 9:1-5 link the items of furniture of the Mosaic sanctuary to "the first covenant."

Our study of covenant in Hebrews, therefore, points to a deep concern with the sin problem and its removal. Both old and new covenants involve respective priesthoods. Each assays to deal with the human predicament. But only one—the new—brings a *decisive* handling of the problem.

So for Hebrews the divisive issues of legalism and grace are foreign to the argument concerning covenant. The apostle discusses two periods of history, two economies of the plan of God. The first, which he calls "the first covenant," centers in the Levitical priesthood and the Old Testament sanctuary and rituals. It cannot finally handle the sin problem *in itself*—that is its deficiency. Only the death of Christ can offer decisive removal of the sins committed under that covenant (see 9:15). Because He is high priest of a totally new order, ministering His own sacrifice in a heavenly tabernacle, he inaugurates a new covenant.

The second idea—access to God—he has hinted at before. Already the apostle had exhorted his Christian readers that, "since then we have a great high priest, . . . let us with confidence draw near to the throne of grace" (4:14-16). Again, he had mentioned that the Melchizedekian priesthood of Jesus brings in "a better hope . . . through which we draw near to God" (7:19).

In the ninth and tenth chapters, however, he amplifies the ideas. The old cultus, he brings out, provided only partial, limited access to God, but the new (in Jesus) has opened the way for all to the presence of God.

The apostle shows the limited access available under the old covenant in 9:1-10. The first five verses give a quick rundown on the items of the earthly Tabernacle. He is not interested in them per se. Nowhere does he come back to them, but he cuts the description short with a curt, "Of these things we cannot now speak in detail." The purpose of 9:1-5 is only to point up the two apartments of the Mosaic Sanctuary, as the following verses indicate. Here we read that the priests have access to "the outer tent" (the holy place) but only the high priest, and that once a year, to "the second" (the most holy place). That he has shaped the account so as to highlight the limited access to God under the old cultus we see by verse 8: "By this the Holy Spirit indicates that the way into the sanctuary [that is, the *real* sanctuary] *is not yet opened* as long as the outer tent is still standing [or, "has a place"—Greek]."

Sometimes Christian writers exalt the nearness of Yahweh to ancient Israel. Those people who heard the word of the living God from Mount Sinai and among whom the Shekinah glory appeared in the wilderness tent—surely they were privileged to have God so close!

But that is not the viewpoint of Hebrews. Rather, it views the Old Testament God as separated by barriers. Common people get no closer than the door of the holy place, priests alone enter the first tent, and one man, on but one day of the year, reaches the actual presence of God. The Sinai experience, furthermore, was one of terror—"blazing fire, and darkness, and gloom, and a tempest, and the sound of a trumpet, and a voice whose words made the hearers entreat that no further messages be spoken to them" (12:18, 19).

In contrast, boldness marks Christianity. By the blood of Jesus New Testament believers enter the sanctuary—the actual presence of God—without fear and trembling.[10] They approach in absolute confidence (10:19-22). Not to Sinai in the desert, but to the heavenly Sinai, city of the living God, celestial Jerusalem, to the assembly of angels and saints they come. And they come through Jesus, Mediator of the new covenant (12:22-24).

Our third idea, conscience, requires close thought. In today's parlance, "conscience" signifies the moral arbiter, the sense of duty, of right and wrong. But let us notice the way in which the apostle uses the term:

9:9, 10: The Old Testament sacrifices could not "perfect the conscience of the worshiper." They were only temporary "regulations for the body."

9:13, 14: Animal blood purifies "the flesh," but the blood of Christ is able to purify the "conscience."

10:1, 2: The very repetition of the Old Testament sacrifices shows that they could not cleanse the "conscience." (Note that the RSV here translates *syneidēsis*, the word elsewhere rendered "conscience," as "consciousness.")

10:22: New Testament believers come to the very presence of God with "hearts sprinkled clean from an evil conscience."

As we study these passages, the following points appear:

1. Throughout, "conscience" has a negative connotation—it has to be "perfected," "purified," or "cleansed."

2. The Old Testament cultus was unable to handle this aspect. Its rituals were external in nature.

3. In contrast, Christ's blood is able to "perfect" or "purify" the "conscience."

Obviously, in Hebrews (and, in fact, elsewhere in the New Testament) "conscience" does not carry the sense of moral referee that we understand by it. Rather, "conscience" here is part of that description of the predicament of man in his sinfulness. It is closer to *consciousness* than to our conscience. A poignant term, it graphically portrays man's "numinous uneasiness." In the words of 10:3, "In these sacrifices there is a reminder of sin year after year." [11]

No *finality* in dealing with sin but a continual *remembrance* of the human predicament, of that defilement which cuts off from the presence of a holy God—an outer purification but an inner *reminding*. Thus the apostle portrays the Old Testament services as they come to focus in the term "conscience."

Now we may better grasp the apostle's use of "imperfection" in terms of the old covenant. We recall that his argument specifically denied "perfection" of the Old Testament priestly system *in itself* (not merely because of its representatives) by the "if" of 7:11 and the categorical "the law made nothing perfect" of 7:19. That imperfection has revealed itself as twofold—in the lack of access to God and the uneasy remembering of sin.

We may save ourselves theological headache if we understand "perfection" in its essential spectrum of meaning. Rather than introducing ideas of sinlessness we should think of *fullness, completeness*. The Old Testament services lacked it. While they were of great value—after all, God ordained them as a way to approach Deity—they were incomplete. They could take the worshiper only so far.

A moment's reflection will convince us of the apostle's point. If the Old Testament services had been altogether adequate in themselves, Christ would have had no need to come. But think of the *weight* of the sin problem, how heavy, as Anselm said it is. If only the blood of bulls and goats could deal with it! One animal, a hundred, a thousand, a million? But no—sin is a *moral* offense, a *religious* one. All the blood of animals that I might muster from slaying cannot atone for it. As the apostle says, "It is *impossible* that the blood of bulls and goats should take away sins" (10:4).

All that the old could not do Christ has done. "For by a single offering he has perfected for all time those who are sanctified" (10:14). As we turn to consider His accomplishment we shall dwell on that "single offering." First we will look at the role of blood in Hebrews 9 and 10.

The Role of Blood

Undoubtedly, "blood" is the key motif of chapters 9 and 10. Of the twenty-one occurrences in Hebrews, fourteen appear here. Nor is the usage a casual one. Over and over the context of the occurrence indicates a highly significant place in the argumentation.

We note, for instance, the threefold expression "not without blood":

9:7: the Aaronic high priest enters the most holy place annually, "not without . . . blood"

9:18: the first covenant was inaugurated, "not . . . without blood"

9:22: no putting away of sins without shedding of blood. The apostle's manner of putting the case serves in a peculiar way to underscore the role of blood.

He builds his thought around three positive statements relative to blood—9:13, 14; 9:22; and 10:4. Let us look at them in turn.

"For if the sprinkling of defiled persons with the blood of goats and bulls and with the ashes of a heifer sanctifies for the purification of the flesh, how much more shall the blood of Christ, who through the eternal Spirit offered himself without blemish to God, purify your conscience from dead works to serve the living God."

The statement summarizes 9:1 to 10:18. It does not reduce the Old Testament sacrificial system to the realm of the superstition of primitive religion, as some students of Hebrews have argued. Rather, it sets out the *limits* of that system—it availed only to "the purification of the *flesh*." That is, it was outward, unable to handle the sin problem decisively. Christ's sacrifice, on the other hand, reaches to the very consciousness, removing sin with finality by His one climactic act. But we note how the discussion turns on *blood*. The argument clearly is from the lesser to the greater—from the blood of animals to the blood of Christ. It is not a "materialistic" Old Testament system (blood) opposed by a "spiritual" New Testament one. The reasoning throughout is cultic and centered in the key term "blood."

"Indeed, under the law almost everything is purified with blood, and without the shedding of blood there is no forgiveness of sins."

The passage, so often quoted, provides the blood axiom that underlies the total reasoning in these chapters. The apostle first refers to "the law," i.e., to the Old Testament ceremonial system. There, blood purified almost everything, though there were occasional exceptions, as when the priests employed fire or water.[12] He passes from the Old Testament to a general statement: "without the shedding of blood there is no forgiveness of sins." Two interesting terms occur here. The first, translated "shedding of blood," appears nowhere else in the New Testament or in other literature until late in the second century. Good evidence suggests that we should better understand it as *"application* of blood" rather then *"shedding* of blood."[13] The second, translated "forgiveness," is unusual in its setting here and may be taken as "release" in the sense of *decisive purification*. That is, the apostle makes both a comparison and contrast through the famous blood rule. We capture his intent by paraphrasing thus: "Under the Old Testament system, almost everything was purified by blood, but for decisive purification it is imperative that blood be applied."

The third text is 10:4: "For it is impossible that the blood of bulls and goats should take away sins." Here the key idea is *take away*. As before, the apostle emphasizes the inability of the Old Testament sacrifices to deal with sin in finality. As his reasoning in 10:1-3 shows, their repetition indicated their ultimate ineffectiveness.

Considering these ideas, we realize that they fall into a clear-cut logical sequence:

Basic Axiom: Purification only by blood (9:22)

    Sub Axiom (1): Animal blood—limited power to purify (9:13)—purifies "the flesh," but cannot decisively remove sin (10:4).

    Sub Axiom (2): Christ's blood—unlimited power to purify (9:14)—purifies even the conscience.

It is clear, then, that the idea of "blood" shapes the thought of Hebrews 9 and 10. Thus, while in chapter 10 he moves from "blood" (10:4) to "body" (10:10) to "sacrifice" and "offering" (10:11-18), he returns quickly to the key term in 10:19: "Therefore, brethren, since we have confidence to enter the sanctuary by the *blood* of Jesus . . ." Likewise, in his subsequent warning against spurning the sacrifice of Christ, he speaks of profaning "the *blood* of the covenant" (10:26-31).

Probably it is impossible to supply a precise equivalent for the term "blood" here. Certainly it stands for more than merely death. Throughout chapters 9 and 10, the apostle keeps the *applying* of blood to the fore. The idea is the pouring out of life in death, of a powerful medium that gathers up defilement *in* itself.

For just as defilement and purification touch religious springs deep within us, so does blood. As mankind in all times and places has sought cleansing from the dirt of sin he has turned to bloody sacrifices. The range of practices is enormous. The sacrificial victims include all forms of life, including human. The benefits sought are diverse. But the human spirit continually testifies that we must pour blood out. And among all the agencies man has sought to purge defilement—water, salt, smoke, oil, and so on—blood has been the preeminent one.

Thus the Book of Hebrews has a universal appeal. Its picture of the numinous unease of mankind—the troubled consciousness—depicts Everyman. And its emphasis on blood as the key agency in the removing of this unease is fundamental to Everyman. Everyman experiences a burden of guilt, a sense of something wrong with his life that only blood can erase.

We are now ready to see the accomplishment of the blood of Christ.

The Accomplishment of Christ

"Blood" is the motif that binds together the ideas of chapters 9 and 10; so the principal point of the apostle is the *better blood* of Christ. As we have seen in the theology of Hebrews the better name, the better priestly order, the better priest, the better tabernacle, and the better covenant, so in its climactic section we come to better blood. Verses 13 and 14 of chapter 9 summarize the idea, as they stress the "how much more" of the blood of Christ.

Throughout Hebrews the blood of Christ has a positive connotation. We may not validly use expressions such as "sin-laden blood" for the apostle's argument. Instead, we see that the blood of Christ is life-giving and hope-giving, accomplishing fully the eternal purpose of God to rescue man from the predicament of sin. Thus, we find:

9:12: Christ gained access to the heavenly tabernacle through His own blood.

9:13, 14: His blood purifies the consciousness.

9:23: It purifies the heavenly sanctuary.

10:19: It provides access for us to the heavenly tabernacle.

10:29: It is the blood of the new covenant.

13:12: He sanctifies (i.e., consecrates) His people through His blood.

The apostle's emphasis in terms of the Old Testament cultus rests on its *repetitive* nature. This, in fact, is the note that sounds throughout the religious history of mankind, with its uneasy sense of defilement. Man, seeking ways to purification,

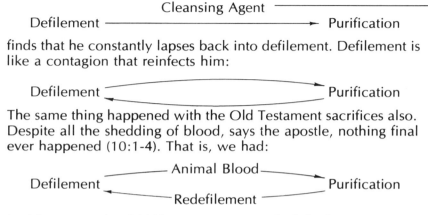

Cleansing Agent

Defilement ———————————————————→ Purification

finds that he constantly lapses back into defilement. Defilement is like a contagion that reinfects him:

Defilement ⟶⟵ Purification

The same thing happened with the Old Testament sacrifices also. Despite all the shedding of blood, says the apostle, nothing final ever happened (10:1-4). That is, we had:

——————— Animal Blood ———————
Defilement ⟶⟵ Purification
——————— Redefilement ———————

In this respect the Old Testament portrayal of the human predicament and attempts to escape it conform to the general religious pattern of mankind.

But now there arises the element of newness. The glad word of Hebrews, the good news of Christianity, proclaims that *the pattern has been broken!* All those attempts to deal with the sin problem, all those multiplied offerings, pilgrimages, penances—no occasion now for them. One Offering has removed the need for any further offering, one Sacrifice has obsoleted all sacrifices, one Blood has succeeded where all blood before fell short. The breaking of the pattern means an irreversible, final solution to the human predicament:

Christ's Blood

Defilement ———————————————————→ Purification

So the new cultus, the heavenly that centers in the blood of Christ, brings "perfecton." We recall the two marks of the old one's inadequacy—its lack of access and its continual reminder of sin. The self-sacrifice of the Son erased both. His blood has rent the veil, opened the inner shrine to the confident believer. And it has forever removed the need for further sacrifice.

These ideas come to beautiful expression in 10:11, 12: "And every priest stands daily at his service, offering repeatedly the

113

same sacrifices, which can never take away sins. But when Christ
had offered for all time a single sacrifice for sins, he sat down at
the right hand of God."

Note the contrasts here:

Old Testament Cultus	*Heavenly Cultus*
Every priest (many)	Christ (*one* priest)
Stands (incomplete)	Sits (complete)
Daily	Single sacrifice
Repeatedly	For all time
Same sacrifices	One sacrifice
Never *take away* sins	An effective sacrifice
His service (earthly Tabernacle)	Right hand of God

No book of the New Testament so exalts the place of Calvary
as does Hebrews. It sets out its message of the finality and
all-sufficiency of the blood of Christ in such striking and
contrasting terms with the Old Testament that every believer may
indeed find absolute confidence.[14]

For our final consideration of this triumphant theme we shall
examine the once-for-all emphasis of the apostle.

Once for All

In five ringing statements the apostle affirms the unique,
irreversible, unrepeatable nature of Calvary:

7:27: "He has no need, like those high priests, to offer
sacrifices daily; . . . he did this *once for all* when he offered up
himself."

9:12: "He entered *once for all* into the Holy Place [better,
"the heavenly sanctuary"], taking . . . his own blood."

9:26: "He has appeared *once for all* . . . to put away sin by
the sacrifice of himself."

9:28: "Christ, having been offered *once* to bear the sins of
many, will appear a second time, *not to deal with sin* but to save
those who are eagerly waiting for him."

10:10: "We have been sanctified [i.e., "consecrated"] through the offering of the body of Jesus Christ *once for all.*"

The apostle's assertions are unequivocal. If we can but allow their significance to permeate our thinking, we will catch a new insight into the centrality of Calvary. We will see its one, eternal, unchanging light, its place as the fulcrum of the ages, its abiding—and present—power to solve the age-old problem of sin.

The apostle shows the all-sufficiency of Calvary by one other means. As we observe his outlining of the Old Testament sacrifices we notice that he constantly alludes to the Day of Atonement, expecially in 9:7, 9:25, and 10:1. And therein lies a problem of interpretation.

The Day of Atonement references have deeply disturbed some SDA students of Hebrews. They have reasoned that Hebrews parallels the Old Testament Yom Kippur ceremonies with the work of Christ on Calvary, thereby indicating that Christ fulfilled His ministry in the most holy place of the heavenly sanctuary at Calvary. Such a conclusion, of course, makes shipwreck of the traditional SDA view of a "first-apartment" work up to 1844 with the "second-apartment" function of judgment—the antitype of the Old Testament Day of Atonement—commencing in 1844. Not surprisingly several students of Hebrews, among whom A. F. Ballenger is best known, have thus eventually parted company with the SDA Church.[15]

The problem and their reaction to it illustrate well a basic principle of Biblical interpretation: *We must put to the text only questions appropriate to its context.* The text is not a computer, as it were, into which we may feed any theological and spiritual inquiries that come into our minds, press the keys, and extract the answers. Each Biblical document is a product of time and place. While the Holy Spirit inspired it, and so it has an enduring significance, the author wrote it in the first place to a particular group of people. The Word of God is always at once the word of man. We may not bypass the historical conditionality of the text. Only as we grasp its own context—what it is talking about, what problems it addresses—may we rightly interpret it.

The fundamental misunderstanding of Hebrews by Ballenger and others lies in putting the wrong questions to the text. The apostle here definitely does *not* deal with the work of Christ in the heavenly tabernacle from a time perspective. What he is concerned with is one supreme idea—*the all-sufficiency of His death*. He contrasts the Old Testament sacrifices with the one Superlative Sacrifice. To do this he takes the high point of the Old Testament religious year—Yom Kippur—and argues that even on this day the sacrifices did not resolve the sin problem, as shown by the annual reenactment of Yom Kippur. That is, the highest point of the Old Testament cultic year could not purge sin away. Obviously, if the Day of Atonement services were inadequate, how much more all other sacrifices.

Christ's own blood, however, accomplished the putting away of sins *with finality*. No more need of sacrifice remains. That once-for-all event surpassed and superseded all the Yom Kippurs of the old cultus. It not only provided decisive purification—even of the uneasy "conscience"—but it flung open the Temple to all. Through His Sacrifice we may come with absolute confidence into the heavenly tabernacle.

The argument of Hebrews, then, does not deny the SDA sanctuary doctrine, because basically it does not address the issue. We may say, particularly on the strength of 9:23, that it allows for it.[16] But we cannot dilute the apostle's emphasis on *one point* in time—the once-for-all sacrifice of Calvary—by importing into the context considerations of subsequent events in history.

The Fourth Basis of Absolute Confidence

"In the cross of Christ I glory,
    Towering o'er the wrecks of time;
All the light of sacred story
    Gathers round its head sublime."

If we have grasped the apostle's reasoning in Hebrews 8 to 10, our Christian life can never be the same again. No more can we doubt and grope, seeking who we are and what we are. Never again can we wonder at the curious riddle of existence, puzzled as to the meaning—if meaning there be—of the enigma of human existence.

For *something* has happened! Calvary is not a figment of the imagination, a pipe dream, or a trance of a visionary. No opponent of Christianity has ever claimed that the cross was an invention of the early Christians. That Jesus was executed on a cross is the most reliable historical datum out of the life of Jesus of Nazareth and is of such a nature that it could not have been a fabrication.

In the cross lay the offense of the new religion. To hail as Messiah the Crucified One was foolishness to Greeks and a stumbling block to Jews.[17] The cross, an object of shame, loathing, humiliation, was a thing of scorn among non-Christians.

But it was *His!* Therein lay the difference. With the thousands of Roman executions over the centuries, one cross was unique. Because Jesus, the Son incarnate, took it up, He transfigured it. The cross as an instrument of torture, a weapon of public execution, deterring the would-be opposer of Rome, could never be the same again. No wonder that it eventually passed out of use.

Non-Christians saw in the cross the failure of the claims of Jesus of Nazareth, but Christians looked and saw there their fulfillment. The cross was the zenith of a life: a cross-life inevitably led to a cross-death. As God's Lamb, born to take away the sin of the world, the death was certain—if He would choose to abide in the divine will.

So Christians have a fixed, immovable base in history. The tides of skepticism and doubt may ebb and flow. Arguments from philosophy and science may rise and fall. Persecution may erupt to coerce the faithful. But that base remains. It is Calvary, the once-for-all Sacrifice for sins.

We encounter an element of deep mystery here. Why, we may ask, did He have to *die?* Was there no other way to expunge the sin problem? But we can give no final answer. We look deep within the plan of God in the Atonement and ultimately encounter mystery. All we can do is to accept the words of

117

Hebrews 9:22 with their axiomatic "blood rule."

The argument of Hebrews, as we have studied it in this chapter, touches every person, whether Christian or not. All of us see ourselves in our most basic sense of religious unease: we are dirty in the presence of the holy God, needing to be washed, to be purged clean. We are troubled and deeply concerned because we are out of harmony with the basic order of the universe. And for this unease, God provides the ultimate answer—blood. He sets forth a cleansing medium that taps deep answering chords within our subconscious. Blood—one efficacious, purifying blood—brings us decisive purification.

The Sacrifice of Christ assures Christians of two great facts: First, the Act *has been done* that solves the sin problem. They don't have to strive and stretch, to hunger and thirst, to press and prevail, in the frantic, frenzied—and futile—effort to find cleansing from their sins. By one sacrifice for all time God has utterly dealt with sin. Nothing we might do can add to that or diminish from it. Calvary gives us absolute confidence of the putting away of sins.[18]

Second, Calvary assures us of our full access to the presence of God. No matter who we might be, we *belong* in Jesus Christ. The gates of the temple stand flung open. All who believe may enter—not cringing, but boldly. We come with "bodies washed" and "hearts sprinkled clean from an evil conscience"—as brothers of the Son incarnate, who died on our behalf.

One last basis of absolute confidence remains. We turn to it for chapter 6.

---

[1] *Macbeth*, Act 5, Scene 1.

[2] A. C. Bouquet, "Numinous Uneasiness," in *Guilt or Pollution and Rites of Purification* (Leiden: Brill, 1968), pp. 1-8.

[3] Matthew 6:12; literally: "Forgive us our debts, as we also have forgiven our debtors."

[4] E.g., reconciliation, adoption, justification, sanctification, liberation.

[5] Boston: Beacon Press, 1969, pp. 25-46.

[6] *Book of the Dead*, chapter 25.

[7] *Ofudesaki*, III, 98.

[8] The volume quoted above (note 2) brings together papers from the congress.

[9] In fact, it is the longest quotation from the Old Testament appearing in the New.

[10] This entry is by "faith," as we shall see later (chapter 7). The apostle is a thoroughgoing supernaturalist. The unseen things are the ultimately real, and faith grasps them.

[11] Was there, therefore, no *personal* assurance in the religion of the Old Testament? Many passages in the Old Testament, especially in the Psalter, would deny the suggestion. We must realize that in Hebrews the apostle presents a capsule view of Israel and her cultus, especially in terms of the annual Day of Atonement. So the *corporate* idea is paramount. We see how different is the concept conveyed by syneidēsis from "conscience."

[12] E.g., Leviticus 5:11-13; Numbers 31:22, 23.

[13] I have argued the case for this in *Defilement and Purgation in the Book of Hebrews,* pp. 323, 324.

[14] We have used the term "blood of Christ" frequently, echoing the language of Hebrews. The term is a religious one of deep significance, one that cannot be simply transposed into rational equivalency. It is noteworthy that the language of Christian worship, shown in hymns and prayers, often reverts to this basic term.

[15] A. F. Ballenger, *Cast Out for the Cross of Christ* (Riverside, California, nd).

[16] Other hints such as the idea of future judgment also furnish support: 9:28; 10:30, 31; 12:25-27.

[17] See 1 Corinthians 1:18-25.

[18] "Our great High Priest completed the sacrificial offering of Himself when He suffered without the gate. Then a perfect atonement was made for the sins of the people. Jesus is our Advocate, our High Priest, our Intercessor. Our present position therefore is like that of the Israelites, standing in the outer court, waiting and looking for that blessed hope, the glorious appearing of our Lord and Saviour Jesus Christ" (Manuscript 128, 1897, in *Seventh-day Adventist Bible Commentary,* Vol. 7A, pp. 663, 664).

"The cross of Calvary challenges, and will finally vanquish, every earthly and hellish power. In the cross all influence centers, and from it all influence goes forth. It is the great center of attraction; for on it Christ gave up His life for the human race" (Manuscript 56, 1899, in *Seventh-day Adventist Bible Commentary,* Vol. 7A, p. 661).

Chapter 6

The King— Ruler Forever

Even in the first century of our era the delay in the Second Coming troubled some Christians. Their Lord had left them, promising to return "quickly." He had given them portents of His coming and had bidden them to watch and be ready. For a while the expectancy ran hot. Among the Thessalonian believers, for instance, some were so sure of the imminent Parousia that they quit working.[1] As the years wore on, however, many Christians began to doubt. Scoffers mocked even the concept of a Second Coming. Christian perplexity over its apparent failure increased.[2]

Clearly, the Hebrews of our study shared this concern. We saw in our opening chapter, as we sketched their spiritual profile, how they had grown weary in the Christian way. The apostle over and over admonished them to hold fast, to be patient, to beware of neglecting or rejecting "so great salvation" (2:3, KJV). But some, we noticed, no longer came to worship services. Some were "wavering," others were "shrinking back" from the promised reward. The relentless passage of the years had made hope grow dim and confidence to slacken.

If His nonreturn in the first generation of the new religion disturbed the followers of Jesus, how much more so after nearly

120

two thousand years of absence. The approach of the third millennium strikes our hearts with bitter poignancy. Our Lord, still apart from us after so long! Surely events have run on in a way undreamed of by the first Christians.

I once heard a famous Jewish scholar remark to a group of Christians, "The problem with your religion is that your history closed two thousand years ago. For us, however, God continues to act in the onward flow of time."

A perceptive observation, it focuses a matter of peculiar import to Protestants—to all Christians, but especially to Protestants—because of their emphasis on Calvary. Bluntly stated, the key question is, *What has happened since Calvary?* If, as the New Testament affirms and Protestants proclaim, Calvary climaxed history, how do we account for those two thousand years? And, of course, in Jewish eyes the very *fact* of those years offers the strongest argument for the non-Messiahship of Jesus of Nazareth. If he had been truly the Messiah, what happened to the kingdom that He announced as being "at hand"?

The passage of the years is an issue that draws in every human being, believer or not. It is, perhaps, *the* essential human issue. With it we confront our frailty, our existential vulnerability. How rapidly our own years fly by! Life, which seems so long in childhood, closes in upon us as we approach maturity. We attempt to shrug off the threat of nothingness that begins to raise its ugly visage, but relentlessly the years roll on. As Gail Sheehy has so well described in her recent *Passages,*[3] by the time of middle age we already are preparing for our death.

Our study of Hebrews so far has raised four pillars for Christian confidence. The Sonship of Jesus, His full humanity, His priesthood, and His all-sufficient sacrifice have directed our gaze away from ourselves to Him. By seeing Him we perceive ourselves—who we are, what we are.

But the problem which we have exposed here we cannot ignore. If those flying years—the fact that they *had* flown—troubled the readers of Hebrews, how much more they bother us. Perhaps our modern world has brought the problem home to us with keener thrust. Not that merely *more* years have passed and the Parousia has not come, though that itself is troublesome. But beyond this, we are probably more conscious of the flow of time. The modern age has brought home to our minds in unparalleled fashion the vast distances of space. And only the infinitudes of time match the infinitudes of distance. We have come to accept mind-boggling numbers of miles and mind-boggling periods of time. Light reaches our little planet from stars so far away that already they are possibly extinct.[4]

No wonder that so many writers of our day have despaired as they contemplated the enigma of existence, the threat of their own nonbeing, the vast emptiness of the universe.[5] Truly, if the apostle is to provide us with a basis for absolute confidence in our age, his sermon must address this fundamental existential issue.

The apostle writes for his time, not ours. While he does not directly speak to the existential question, he has much of an indirect nature. We may, I think, detect three main lines of argument by which he seeks to reassure those readers concerned by the delay in the Return. We will take up each in order and then consider their helpfulness to our situation.

The Promise Reiterated

His obvious approach is to reiterate the promise. "Christ, . . . offered once to bear the sins of many, *will appear a second time*," he reminds them (9:28). Although some Christians grow tired in their religion and don't bother to go to church anymore, the Hebrews are to mutually exhort to love and good works. He told them, Encourage "one another, and all the more *as you see the Day drawing near*" (10:24, 25).

So the apostle knows no theological legerdemain which will annul the Second Coming. For him it is a part of the Christian world view and can be stated without explanation or apology. If the Lord has not come as soon as some Christians expected, that in no way can remove the primitive teaching of the religion—rather, the Day must have drawn so much the nearer.

In two places—both as we might expect, among the

122

exhortations of Hebrews—he quotes Scripture in support of the promise of the Second Coming. The content of the first, 10:35-39, shows us the *practical* nature of his argument. "Therefore do not throw away your confidence, which has a great reward. For you have need of endurance, so that you may do the will of God and receive what is promised.

'For yet a little while,
and the coming one shall come and shall not tarry;
but my righteous one shall live by faith,
and if he shrinks back,
my soul has no pleasure in him.'

"But we are not of those who shrink back and are destroyed, but of those who have faith and keep their souls."

We see here: (1) the *certainty* of the promise—as definite as Scripture that He "shall not tarry"; (2) the *nearness* of the promise—in "a little while"; and (3) the correct *response* to the promise—endurance instead of shrinking back.

The second passage strikes a stern chord. Here in 12:25-29, the promise of the Return appears in the context of judgment: "See that you do not refuse him who is speaking. For if they did not escape when they refused him who warned them on earth, much less shall we escape if we reject him who warns from heaven. His voice then shook the earth; but now he has promised, 'Yet once more I will shake not only the earth but also the heaven.' This phrase, 'Yet once more,' indicates the removal of what is shaken, as of what has been made, in order that what cannot be shaken may remain. Therefore let us be grateful for receiving a kingdom that cannot be shaken, and thus let us offer to God acceptable worship, with reverence and awe; for our God is a consuming fire." The passage elaborates the last words of 10:39—those who "*keep their souls.*"

So the apostle reiterates the promise of the Second Coming without theological elaboration. For him the problem is not theological but personal and spiritual. He sees, as it were, two responses to the *fact* of the promise of the Return:

Response 1 (undesirable): weariness, doubt, sporadic church attendance, shrinking back to the way of the world. It needs reminding of the certainty of divine judgment on those who refuse to heed the warnings of God.

Response 2 (desirable): confidence in the promise, endurance, mutual encouragement of the Return's drawing near, faith. Result: eternal salvation.

This line of argument still appeals to many Christians. For them it is sufficient that the promise of the Parousia is a clear Biblical doctrine. Their concern is not to question the long delay in the fulfillment of the promise but to apply it to personal Christian living.

Other Christians need more. They would argue that the relentless passage of the years forces us to think about the promise, to consider if we should understand it in a different way, or whether it still can be taken seriously. Not surprisingly, then, in many Christian bodies the doctrine of the Second Coming has long since ceased to attract serious consideration. While they may mouth the words as part of the early Christian creed, the belief in a personal, literal return of Christ has passed into oblivion, crushed by the tramp of the years.

And for non-Christians, the mere reiteration of the promise carries no weight whatsoever. The idea of the Second Coming represented only a gush of early apocalyptic thought, long since proved—by the years—to have been misguided.

The apostle's reasoning in Hebrews, however, opens up two other lines of argument that bear on the problem of the delay. The first centers in his concept of the "real."

The "Real" and the Visible

Let us make no mistake about it—the apostle holds to the reality of the present world. It was, he says, created through the Son (1:2)—an act grasped only by faith (11:3). That same Son upholds the universe by the word of His power (1:3). And the Second Coming will shake the present order of creation to its foundations, as we have just noticed (12:25-29). Thus any philosophy that denies the substantiality of the world—such as classical Hinduism's teaching of *maya* (illusion)—will not do.

124

Yet the apostle's thought is more complex. He is not a materialist. While he affirms the reality of the universe as we see and know it, he introduces talk of the "real" beyond the universe we perceive. He contrasts what we call the "real" (the universe) with what is the *really* real (and which he terms the "real").

We saw such a distinction made in his discussion of the heavenly sanctuary. He did not deny the existence of the earthly, hence his brief description of it in 9:1-5, but he rejects that it is the "real." God, not man, set up the "real" or genuine tabernacle (8:2). It is "the greater and more perfect tent (not made with hands, that is, *not of this creation*)" (9:11). What we call the "real"—the earthly—was but a copy and shadow of the really real (8:5; 9:23; 10:1).

An interesting concept of reality emerges. The apostle holds to two separate, parallel "creations," that is, orders of creation or existence. All that we see and know, the empirical world so well measured and probed by science and increasingly subject to the technology of science—*our* world—is not the highest reality. While it is not a figment of the mind, it is not the ultimate. Our world is the world of man. The "real" is the world of God.

Such a view is, of course, not uncommon. Plato's teaching of the "Ideal" approximates to it.[6] The apostle's conception, however, breaks the Greek pattern. We saw in the last two chapters his strong concern with events *in time*. That is, he does not hold to two eternally distinct orders, the lower (ours) being time-bound and the upper (the Ideal or real) being timeless. Instead, the spatial idea of two worlds (creations) is crossed by the temporal one. So we saw that the *real* tabernacle comes into its own in time, that access to it *becomes* available only after Calvary (9:8, 9).

The apostle's distinction of the "real" and "really real" reemerges in the closing chapters of Hebrews. As he applies the theological development that climaxed and concluded in the passage ending at 10:18, he encourages his hearers to steadfastness by distinguishing the visible from the invisible. Over and over he makes his point: the visible is but temporary, the invisible is ultimate reality. Notice how often the idea surfaces:

11:3: The universe, which is visible, has its origin in the invisible. That is, the invisible is prior to, and greater than, the seen world.

11:6: The primacy of faith—we do not determine God's existence by sensory perception. Thus, the Supreme Reality belongs to the realm of the invisible.

11:7: We have the example of Noah, who heeded divine warnings regarding events yet unseen and so was saved.

11:8: Abraham, following the call of God, went out with no knowledge of destination.

11:10: His hope was of a *real* city, one "which has foundations, *whose builder and maker is God.*" Here we see exact parallelism with the description of the heavenly tabernacle.

11:11: Sarah's faith in the ability of God to do the impossible under the present creation led to the birth of Isaac.

11:13-16: A summary of the hope of the patriarchs—they did not receive "the promises" on this earth but sought "a homeland, . . . a *better* country, that is, a *heavenly* one. Therefore God is not ashamed to be called their God, *for he has prepared for them a city.*"

11:19: Abraham had faith in God's ability to raise even the dead to life.

11:20-22: Isaac, Jacob, and Joseph all looked *to the future* for the realization of the promise.

11:26, 27: Moses forsook the treasures of Egypt as he *"looked to the reward"*—the future homeland of the people of God. Likewise, "he endured *as seeing him who* is invisible."

11:39, 40: The heroes of faith believed God's promise but did not receive it.

12:1, 2: Christians are to run the race of life, "looking to Jesus," i.e., "as seeing him who is invisible."

12:22-24: Christians see by faith the "real" city, the heavenly Jerusalem, with its assembly of the saved.

13:14: In an echo of 11:10, 16, the apostle reminds the Hebrews that they have "no lasting city" in this world, but instead, they "seek *the city which is to come.*"

The thrust is clear. Whether Old Testament or New, the

people of God are characterized by their *seeing the invisible,* which is the *really* real, because it is of God. They seek for a city, a homeland, but not of the present order. Like the heavenly tabernacle, its maker is God, so it is lasting and genuine but not accessible to sensory perception.[7]

As with the apostle's argument regarding the heavenly sanctuary, a temporal concept crosses the spatial one. While God *has prepared* the heavenly city (11:16), the people of God *look forward* to it (11:10), *desire* it (11:16), *seek* it (13:14). So it is "the city *which is to come*" (13:14).

It is apparent that with these ideas we have quite a different way of handling the delay in the Parousia. Instead of a repetition of the promise of the Return, the apostle introduces us to a whole new picture of reality. The concept of two parallel creations, with the "really real" separate, coexistent, and invisible, radically modifies the purely linear (historical) reference. Now *what already is* guarantees the future. That is, the heavenly city is "to come" because it already exists in the invisible world. As that world is *the* real, the genuine, the everlasting, so the winding up of human history is sure.

We come now to the third way in which the Book of Hebrews sheds light on the existential problem, centering in the idea of Christ as King.

The King

The third verse of the sermon to the Hebrews states that the Son, after His work of making purgation of sins, "sat down at the right hand of the Majesty on high." In three other places—1:13, 8:1, and 10:12—the apostle returns to the idea of Christ as King. The words are based on Psalm 110:1, but the idea remains undeveloped in Hebrews. Instead of the royal role, the apostle emphasizes Christ's *priestly* function. Thus instead of the first verse of Psalm 110, it is the fourth, with its prediction of the rise of a Melchizedekian priest, that shapes the argument. [8]

The four allusions to the regnant Son call for consideration, however. They obviously bear directly upon the question of this chapter. How can the apostle portray Christ as *ruling* when so many spurn the idea of His Lordship?

As we study the references in Hebrews to Christ as King, we note a significant qualification. The psalm itself (110:1) calls the Son to sit at the place of honor *"till* I make thy enemies a stool for thy feet"* (1:13). In the allusion in chapter 10 the apostle underscores the point (though without elaboration): "But when Christ had offered for all time a single sacrifice for sins, he sat down at the right hand of God, *then to wait until his enemies should be made a stool for his feet"* (10:12, 13).

So a tension arises here. Christ *is* King but is not yet fully *acknowledged* as King. The author of Hebrews balances what He *has* accomplished, what He now *is,* and what is yet *to be.* The flow of history cannot alter what He already has done—the One Sacrifice, once for all. Nothing can add to or diminish its superlative worth. Nor can the years as they roll change His status. He is the Son, once incarnated, now exalted and reigning. What the passage of the years can bring is but the full recognition of His act and His person.

We catch the significance of the apostle's words in his references to time. In the previous chapter we saw the weight that hangs on the phrase "once for all" and do not need to recapitulate it. Two other references concern us here. The first appears at the opening of his sermon. After mentioning the speaking of God in the Old Testament, he states that *"in these last days* [or possibly, "in the last of these days"—i.e., the days of revelation] he has spoken to us by a Son." Let us put the second passage with it: "He has appeared once and for all *at the climax of history* to abolish sin by the sacrifice of himself" (9:26, NEB).

The apostle's philosophy of history is unmistakable. For him, all history before Calvary only prepared for that event. The cross, the climax of history, rent time asunder. With Christ's accomplishment there, "these last days" (or "the final age" as the NEB translates 1:2) commenced. This age is the time of waiting until the divine will is fully worked out, which will be when the entire universe shall bow in acknowledgment of Christ as King.

So the Christian lives in a curious relationship to time. On the one hand he looks *back* to an event that is the midpoint of history. The cross has determined the course of the future, the certain, eventual triumph of the reign of the good and the removal of evil. On the other, he looks *ahead* to the consummation, to the day when He who is King by right will be King indeed.[9]

We find the balancing of the "already" of Calvary with the "not yet" of the Parousia stamped on all New Testament thought.[10] The Book of Hebrews in this respect reflects typical New Testament eschatology. But a question immediately raises its head: When one looks either to the past or to the future, what happens to the *present?* Is not this issue in fact at the root of the present malaise in Christendom? Protestants face two alternatives. Either the hope of the Return has faded away and they have only a *backward*-looking philosophy of history, or—considering the Parousia still a live option—they hang suspended between the times, as it were, looking back two thousand years and hoping against hope to God's V-day, ever conscious of the relentless passage of the years.

The apostle of our sermon now steps in to make his unique contribution. He introduces a concept that bridges the gap between Calvary and the Return. Yes, he says, Calvary is the climax of the ages. Its Sacrifice is efficacious to deal with sins once for all. We must never reduce the magnificent *Already* of the work of our Lord. But, as Christians, we have not only the "already" and the "not yet" but the "now"—Jesus is our High Priest. Because He is our Sympathetic Mediator as well as King awaiting the realization of the kingdom in its fullness, the present is filled with meaning. The waiting time between cross and Parousia is also the period of heavenly high priesthood.

The apostle does not tell us the precise nature of Christ's priestly activity. "He always lives to make intercession," he tersely sums it up (7:25). We may be sure, on the basis of our studies in Hebrews so far, as well as other data in the New Testament, that he does not suggest that God is *reluctant* to receive sinners, nor does he want to add anything to the Act of Calvary. Rather, Christ's mediatorial work is *by virtue of* His

Sacrifice, once accomplished for all. He ministers its *benefits*.

Thus, throughout Hebrews the accent falls on the now time. While the hope of the Parousia remains, we are not to let it trouble us by its delay. We now "*have* a great high priest who has passed through the heavens, Jesus, the Son of God. . . . Let us then with confidence *draw near* to the throne of grace" (4:14-16). "It was fitting that we *should have* such a high priest, holy, blameless, unstained, separated from sinners, exalted above the heavens. . . . We *have* such a high priest, one who is seated at the right hand of the throne of the Majesty in heaven" (7:26-8:1). "Therefore, brethren, since we have confidence *to enter* the sanctuary by the blood of Jesus, . . . and since we have a great priest over the house of God, let us *draw near* with a true heart in full assurance of faith" (10:19-22). "You *have come* to Mount Zion and to the city of the living God, the heavenly Jerusalem, . . . and to Jesus, the mediator of a new covenant" (12: 22-24).

So the future grows out of the now time as well as the past (Calvary). The present blessings of the Christian religion temper the delay in the Parousia. The future resonates with the now.

This interaction of present and future offers the key to a much-debated passage of the book—4:1-11—with its cryptic message: "So then, there remains a sabbath rest for the people of God" (4:9). The discussion really begins much earlier, in 3:6b. Throughout 3:7-19 the apostle draws a lesson from the wandering people of God in the Old Testament. Although God had promised them the inheritance of Canaan, they failed because of unbelief. For forty years they roamed the desert until at last all perished. In chapter 4 the apostle jumps to Christians of his day—his readers. They too have received the promise of rest, but they too may fail unless faith mixes with the Good News.

The vital issues of interpreting 4:1-11 are: (1) What is the "rest" that remains for God's people? (2) When will they enter it—now or in the future? (3) How does the Sabbath figure in the argument? We cannot here embark upon an exegesis of the passage, but will merely seek to show how the reasoning combines both present and future elements. On the one hand, the apostle uses present tenses: "We who have believed enter that rest. . . . Whoever enters God's rest also ceases from his labors" (4:3-10). Yet the background of the passage, in 3:7-19, is definitely future-directed. As the Israelites of old failed to enter earthly Canaan, so his readers may fail to enter the heavenly Canaan. Hence 4:11—"Let us therefore strive to enter that rest, that no one fall by the same sort of disobedience."

Likewise with the Sabbath allusion. Whereas he employs a single word for "rest" (Greek: *katapausis*) throughout chapters 3 and 4, at 4:9 he introduces a new word, *sabbatismos* ("sabbath rest," "sabbathlike rest").[11] He can do this because he has earlier (4:3, 4) mentioned the Sabbath to show the *availability* of the divine rest (i.e., no failure on God's part to provide the "rest"). Now the Sabbath itself carries a twofold aspect of present and future. On the one hand, it illustrates that rest of the people of God who trust wholly on the merit of Calvary and cease from their own works. On the other, it points forward to that perfect rest of the eternal order, as the rabbis said, "The people of Israel said, 'Lord of the whole world, show us the world to come.' God, blessed be He, answered, 'Such is the pattern of the Sabbath.' "[12]

The "rest" of 4:1-11, then, Christians enter *now*, but realize it in its fullness only at the Parousia. Of it the Sabbath is both part and representation. Here we have come full circle. The aspect of Christ as King has merged with that of the "real," the invisible, which we met above.

While He has not attained full rule yet, He is now *seated*. That seating carries with it deep significance for the now time. It enables Christians to anticipate the heavenly goal as they await its realization.

Hebrews and Our Day

Let us take up in turn the three responses of Hebrews to the delay in the Parousia. How helpful are they to modern Christians and modern man?

We spoke briefly above about reactions to the appeal to Scripture. A few words more seem necessary—and here we have in mind Christian readers (the non-Christian obviously can find no pause for thought in this). It is impossible to deny or downplay the place of apocalyptic in the thought of the New Testament. Albert Schweitzer, in his monumental *The Quest of the Historical Jesus,* [13] placed the Founder of Christianity firmly in the apocalyptic mold (although his portrayal has exaggerated elements), and New Testament scholarship since Schweitzer has shown the crucial role of apocalyptic thought in shaping New Testament thinking.

We cannot lightly brush aside the New Testament teaching of the Second Coming. In one way or another we must come to terms with it. Perhaps we may decide at last that the idea is outmoded, misguided—this must surely carry serious implications for our view of the entire canon. Or we may decide that the idea is still a theological option. Then we must wrestle with it as modern thinkers.

Thus the apostle's reiteration of the promise of the Parousia challenges us to serious reflection. It confronts us with that first-century milieu, that cradle of our religion. And it helps us to see—by contrast—our twentieth-century world and ourselves as part of it.

The second line of reasoning we pursued calls into question the prevailing world view. In a curious way it *allows for* the empirical world—that world so familiar to us as the scientific method has held sway for more than two hundred years. The apostle's picture of the two parallel "creations" (orders) affords reality and meaning to the world we know. But it drastically shifts the philosophical focus by challenging the *sufficiency* of the empirical world view. It purports that the *really* real lies outside and beyond our world, eluding the grasp of the scientist. Sensory evidence it affords second, instead of prior, place.

Another way of stating the issue is in terms of "natural" and "supernatural." The Book of Hebrews affirms the *fact* and *superiority* of the supernatural—it alone is the ultimate real.

The Book of Hebrews has thrown the gauntlet down. Nearly three centuries of modern thought must rise up in savage rejoinder.

Strangely enough, recent currents of Western thought are

more susceptible to the view of Hebrews. The 1960s saw a turning from science and its technology, even—on the part of some—a repudiation of all it stood for. Western man has become fed up with the objective, dispassionate stance of the empirical method. More and more he looks within himself to find the secret of existence.

With all our vaunted progress man still feels dissatisfied. When he has been weighed, analyzed, and explained, after he has been dissected and discussed, he is still frustrated. There is something *more*. Something beyond objective study. His aesthetic sensibilities whisper it to him, his moral judgments repeat it, his insatiable hunger to ground his being in something—in what he may not know—shouts out for it.

In Christian terms he is looking for God and the world of the "real."

If the second argument of Hebrews seems to speak with special power to modern man, alone and apart from God, the third has particular appeal to Christians.

Our hope in the Return is not a blind optimism. It is based on a happening. One event in time has sealed the future and made it certain beyond all question. Because the Son now sits at the right hand of the Majesty in the heavens, all the universe must one day come to bow at His feet and acknowledge His Lordship. With Hebrews so positive in its message of Calvary, the promise of the Parousia rings with absolute confidence.

But ours is not an idle waiting, a fervent expectation for things to improve. Every present moment has meaning. Even now our Lord is High Priest in the "real" world, mediating on our behalf and sympathetic to every need, every struggle, every test. And even now the doors of that temple above stand wide open for us. By faith we draw near, in full assurance of purification of our sins and our welcome home.

The foundation for absolute confidence is now complete. Five bases—Sonship, Brotherhood, High Priesthood, Sacrifice, and Kingship—make it impregnable. Understanding them, grasping them, appropriating them to ourselves, we find out *who* we are, *what* we are, and *where* we are in the riddle of human existence.

The Good News according to Hebrews is the "such a great salvation" of which the apostle spoke. It is the message that brought hope and assurance to Christians nearly two thousand years ago.

And it is still Good News! We too need to know it, to remind ourselves of it. Today we too need the absolute confidence that comes in its wake.

But what shall we *do* with it? What might the Hebrews do with it? Or, we may say, if the five pillars show us the *what* of the Gospel, then *so what?*

Another way of stating the matter is in terms of the *nature* of absolute confidence. The five bases we have studied so far supply the theological foundation, but how will such absolute confidence work out in everyday living? The following chapter will take up this matter.

---

[1] See 2 Thessalonians 3:6-12. Apparently the believers had misunderstood Paul's counsel in 1 Thessalonians to mean that the Parousia was imminent (see 1 Thessalonians 4:13-5:11).

[2] Scoffers are explicitly mentioned in 2 Peter 3:3-15. This letter is written to Christians troubled by the passage of time.

[3] Gail Sheehy, *Passages: Predictable Crises of Adult Life* (New York: E. P. Dutton & Co., Inc., 1976).

[4] It is perhaps man's conquest of *space* in the modern era which has thrown into sharp relief his vulnerability in *time*.

[5] Much of the great writing of our century is in this vein: Kafka, Sartre, Camus, Hemingway.

[6] In fact, the two-dimensional cosmology (the earthly having a heavenly counterpart) was widespread in the ancient East.

[7] Cf 2 Corinthians 4:17, 18: "For this slight momentary affliction is preparing for us an eternal weight of glory beyond all comparison, because we look not to the things that are seen but to the things that are unseen; for the things that are seen are transient, but the things that are unseen are eternal."

[8] The description of Melchizedek as king of righteousness and king of peace (Hebrews 7:1, 2) would have provided an easy introduction to a discussion of Jesus as king. We have seen, however, that chapter 7, in keeping with the theological interest of the sermon, takes up only the priestly aspect.

[9] Professor Oscar Cullmann in various writings has underscored the cross as the midpoint of time. See especially his *Salvation in History*. (London: SCM, 1967).

[10] In the Synoptic Gospels, the "kingdom" motif; in Revelation, the "Lamb"

and "judgment" motifs; in Acts and the Pauline letters, the "Spirit" and "Parousia" motifs.

[11] In fact, we do not find the word *sabbatismos* before this occurrence. It ispossible—even likely—that he has coined it.

[12] *Jalk, Rub.* 95, 4.

[13] Albert Schweitzer, *The Quest of the Historical Jesus: A Critical Study of Its Progress from Reimarus to Wrede* (New York: Macmillan, 1948).

Chapter 7

The Nature of Absolute Confidence

It is one thing to understand theology. To live it is the more difficult task. Not that the two have no relationship. From the beginning of our study of Hebrews we saw the weight the apostle gives to theological argument.[1] We must lay a theological foundation, but that is only the beginning. A superstructure of Christian living must rise upon that. So the ultimate purpose of Hebrews is homiletical. Absolute confidence, established on the five theological pillars, reveals itself in the nitty-gritty of life.

Once again, then, we turn to the exhortations of Hebrews. At the outset we saw the twin dangers that threatened the Hebrews: those of neglect and rejection of the "great salvation" offered in Jesus the Son. Having elaborated the privileges of the Christian religion in the theological sections, the apostle now drives home his message in unmistakable clarity. The "what" of the gospel calls for a corresponding "so what" in practical living. Clearly, absolute confidence will not be brash or presumptuous. The "great salvation" will not ride roughshod over ethics. The sacrifice of Calvary will not place the believer in a state of immunity to sin and failure.

As we look once more to the exhortations, we notice a

twofold division. On one hand, the apostle, alert to the perils of neglect and rejection, counsels to *positive* Christian living. On the other, he gives *negative* advice in the form of strongly worded warnings. By studying both aspects we will better grasp how the Christian lives in absolute confidence in the salvation offered by Jesus the Son.

The Positive Response

The apostle laces his exhortations with positive vocabulary. Let us list his advice, bearing in mind that each term represents a different word in the original text:

to pay attention, give heed to, be alert	(2:1)
to hold fast	(3:6, 14; 10:23)
to grasp, hold fast, to seize	(4:14; 6:18)
to strive, to show earnestness	(4:11; 6:11)
to consider	(3:1)
to exhort, to encourage, to urge, to appeal	(3:13, 10:25; 13:19, 22)
to recall	(10:32)
to imitate those with faith and patience	(6:12)
to have endurance, patience, perseverance, hope	(10:36; 12:1; 3:6; 6:11, 18; 10:23)
to possess courage, confidence, boldness	(3:6; 4:16; 10:19, 35)
to hold fast our confession, profession	(3:1; 4:14; 10:23)
to be firm, permanent, reliable, valid, steadfast	(2:2; 3:6, 14; 6:19)

One term—"faith"—takes pride of place over all of them, however. Its various forms surface no fewer than forty-one times, while the manner in which it enters the writing shows its role as a key idea. (Have not Christians over the centuries always turned to Hebrews 11 as "the faith chapter" of the Bible?) We do well to study it carefully. Perhaps we shall find more in this familiar term than we have thought.

First of all in our study of faith, we need to recognize the problems caused by translations into English of the Greek terms. While we may make distinctions in meaning between "faith" and "belief," only one word underlies the Greek—*pistis*. The same root, in the verb form, signifies "to have faith," "to believe," while as an adjective it indicates "faithful," "believing." A negative form of the noun is *apistia,* i.e., "unfaith," or "unbelief."

The first group of occurrences of the *pistis* terminology comes in chapter 3. It is the adjective "faithful," introduced at 2:17, that shapes the discussion in 3:1-6a. As we noticed in our study of Jesus as High Priest, the apostle here links Moses to Jesus by the characteristic of faithfulness. From 3:6b to 19 the apostle rings another change on the *pistis* root. He warns the Hebrew Christians against "an evil, unbelieving [*un*faithful] heart" (3:12) and locates the failure of the wilderness generation squarely at this point: "So we see that they were unable to enter because of unbelief [literally: unfaith]" (3:19).

If *un*faith, or lack of faith, was the worm in the apple of ancient Israel's religion, then should not the readers of his letter seek to have *faith?* That is where we would expect the logic to lead, and 4:1-11 shows this very idea. The Good News came to the wilderness people, he tells them, but it did not profit them, because it met no answering chord of faith (4:2). But *we who believe*—we who have faith—enter God's rest (4:3).

His reasoning in chapters 3 and 4 confirms our earlier remarks as to his purpose in writing to the Hebrews. He wants them first of all to hear the Good News in its grandeur of the Son as Priest and Sacrifice, if not for the first time. But he wants them to respond *in faith* to that message so that it may benefit them. The gospel in itself is not sufficient.[2] It presents God's side, all that He has done in taking the initiative to solve the human predicament. Unless man responds positively to it, however, it falls short. God does not *coerce* man by the gospel. The Lord does not manipulate the mind, despite (and surely, because of) His love for man. Unless man puts his will on the side of God, the good seed of the gospel falls barren upon the ground.

But what does the apostle mean by his call for "faith" here? Is he exhorting the Hebrews to an acceptance of the Good News, to an initial response of trust in the primitive Christian message?

Obviously not. Our studies early showed us that the Hebrews already were Christians. Their problem was not so much *becoming* Christian, but *continuing* as Christian. They had grown weary in the way, just as the Israelites fell away in the wilderness. What we are dealing with is, negatively, the problem of *un*faith, which is a gradual, continuous matter, and positively, with faith, which also is a matter of constancy in Christian living. So we notice again 4:1-11: The apostle can say that by *faith* we enter God's rest (4:3) and in the next breath that we should *"strive* to enter that rest" (4:11).

It is clear, then, that the apostle's sermon does not relegate "faith" to simply a single act of acceptance of God's salvation. Nor is it a matter of mental assent to theological teaching. No—faith is practical, continuous, constant to the end.

We see these ideas brought out sharply in 6:11, 12: "And we desire each one of you to show the same earnestness in realizing the full assurance of hope until the end, so that you may not be sluggish, but imitators of those who through faith and patience inherit the promises." Notice the emphases here: Faith keeps company with earnestness, assurance, hope, and patience. It is "the end" that is the goal, when the promises will be realized. The enemy of faith is sluggishness. So the *enduring* quality of faith a la Hebrews stands out boldly.

The passage, in fact, anticipates the final group of *pistis* references. At 6:12 the apostle admonished imitation of the people of faith, an idea whose practical value was—and is—too helpful to pass by lightly. Chapter 11 almost wholly consists of a listing of such examples of faith and patience, with the refrain "by faith" coming eighteen times and structuring the whole.

The final group of references to faith, however, begins at 10:22. We have come to know the verse well, with its triumphant note of "full assurance of faith." At 10:37, 38 the apostle quotes Habakkuk 2:3, 4 to reaffirm the certainty of the promise of the Second Coming. The second part of the citation provides the formula for life in the waiting time: "My righteous one shall *live* by faith."[3] So the admonition of verse 39: "We are not of those who shrink back and are destroyed, but of *those who have faith and keep their souls.''*

The verses confirm our observations about *pistis* based on the earlier occurrences. Faith is not so much an act of decision as a way of life. The absolute confidence of Christians is *in faith.* They live *by faith* as they wait for the Return. Because *of faith* they avoid the peril of shrinking back, and they attain the goal of final salvation.

So we come to chapter 11, which we may fairly see as a filling out of the content of the faith references we just noticed in 10:22, 37-39. That is, the apostle will illustrate what it means in practice to have the full assurance of faith, to live by faith, to have faith to the end. In this chapter, *pistis* will no longer be a subsidiary term but will move to center stage.

He commences with a twofold designation of faith itself. Faith, he says, is *assurance* and conviction of the unseen. The first word, translated ''assurance'' in the RSV and ''substance'' in the KJV, indicated property-rights, as we know from an archaeological find. In a land dispute in ancient Egypt, a noble woman sent documents supporting her claim to the magistrate. A servant carried them in an earthen vessel. On the way he lodged at an inn, which burned in the night. What became of him we do not know, but the documents survived till their recent discovery. They reveal the title deed to the land. Thus we may understand Hebrews 11:1: ''Faith is the title deed of things hoped for, the conviction of things not seen.''

Suppose one day we receive a surprising letter in the mail. Our long-forgotten Aunt Agatha has died, willing her estate in Hawaii to us. Now, we have never been to Hawaii—we have never seen the property—but it is ours. It is as good as the word of the law.

So with faith. It lays hold on that invisible order, that real world, which Hebrews sets forth. Although we do not now see that ''homeland,'' that ''city,'' by faith we know it to exist, to be sure and certain.

Faith, then, is a human characteristic,[4] but it is not like the senses. It touches the untouchable, sees the unseeable, hears the sound of silence. And, as the apostle quickly reminds us, it *keeps on* doing all these things. Without wavering, it knows that the inheritance is fail-safe—because it itself is the title deed.

The apostle now proceeds on a long list of examples. From the Creation to his day, the people of God have borne the stamp "by faith." Many and varied are their exploits—acceptable sacrifice, translation, deliverance from the Deluge, wanderers in strange lands, childbirth in old age, abdication of the throne, deliverance from foreign bondage, the Exodus. In verses 32 to 38 his mind runs down the list of worthies from the Old Testament to his own time, the characters crowding one upon another until the account surges to its climax:

"And what more shall I say? For time would fail me to tell of Gideon, Barak, Samson, Jephthah, of David and Samuel and the prophets—who through faith conquered kingdoms, enforced justice, received promises, stopped the mouths of lions, quenched raging fire, escaped the edge of the sword, won strength out of weakness, became mighty in war, put foreign armies to flight. Women received their dead by resurrection. Some were tortured, refusing to accept release, that they might rise again to a better life. Others suffered mocking and scourging, and even chains and imprisonment. They were stoned, they were sawn in two, they were killed with the sword; they went about in skins of sheep and goats, destitute, afflicted, ill-treated—of whom the world was not worthy—wandering over deserts and mountains, and in dens and caves of the earth."

As we look over chapter 11 we see clearly that *pistis* has two principal aspects—it sees the invisible, and it endures.

We have noticed the first above in our discussion of "assurance" as title deed. Over and over the apostle comes back to the point, however. None of those he mentions could see, *at the time* of his exploit, the result. Each acted by faith, i.e., by assurance from the invisible world. Abel offers sacrifice—and God accepts it. Enoch lives a holy life—and the Lord translates him. Noah builds an ark—and saves his household. Abraham went out from Ur—and found the Promised Land. Sarah was old and barren—but conceived. Abraham offered up Isaac—and

141

received his son again. Moses forsook the throne—and led the people out from Egypt. The Israelites entered the Red Sea—and crossed it. They marched around Jericho—and the walls fell down. Rahab sheltered the spies—and saved her own life.

The second aspect looks to the *future*. Faith keeps on, is steadfast. It acts *now* out of its conviction of the "real," but is confident that God's tomorrow will vindicate the present act. The life of faith looks forward "to the city which has foundations, whose builder and maker is God" (11:10). All the heroes and heroines of old "died in faith, not having received what was promised, but having seen it and greeted it from afar, and having acknowledged that they were strangers and exiles on the earth" (11:13; see 11:39 also).

Both aspects—the claim to the invisible and steadfastness—flow together and throughout the chapter. In the sixth verse, however, we may distinguish them: "Without faith it is impossible to please him. For whoever would draw near to God must believe that he exists and that he rewards those who seek him" Here we first meet the indispensability of faith—without it it is impossible to please God. Verse 39 indicates that those mentioned received recognition because of their faith. Then we see faith as conviction of the invisible—the seeker after God must have faith that He exists. Finally, we detect the enduring, future-directed aspect—faith looks to the invisible God, who will *reward* those who seek Him.

We are now ready to crystallize our concept of faith in Hebrews. Faith is an *assurance of the invisible world that perseveres to the end*.

Unfortunately, students of the Bible often flit like butterflies from one book to another. While one should study all the Word, we need to recognize the particular theological contribution of each document. The scattershot approach to Bible study tends to blur the differentiations *within* the New Testament. Instead of a rainbow we have a generalized, gray theology.

If we look carefully at the New Testament, we discern that faith is a diamond with many facets. While its core idea is trust in God, individual books and passages turn faith in the light to reveal its full beauty. In Romans and Galatians, for instance, the context opposes human efforts to attain salvation with God's free gift. Faith is acceptance of the gift—the renouncing of the human ability and the taking of God at His word.[5] In James, however, faith's intellectual aspect comes to the fore. Here even the demons believe, or have faith. That is, they know of the reality of God.[6]

Hebrews turns the diamond once more in the light. Now we see the assurance, the conviction, of the unseen world, that it is the "real," not the one proclaimed by our senses. And with this assurance comes the element of perseverance, lifelong continuance in the conviction of the unseen. Faith in Hebrews is close to *faithfulness.*[7]

If theology, then, gives the bases of absolute confidence, that confidence is to be lived *in faith.* Christians are to be steadfast, to persevere to the end. Their reward is sure. Faith is its title deed and it already is in the "real" world.

We turn now to study the apostle's severe warnings.

The Negative Response

Early in our investigation of Hebrews we saw that the Hebrew Christians faced spiritual hazards. The insidious cancer of neglect, the subtle hardening of the spiritual arteries, the deceitful inroads of sin, the tragedy of stunted growth, the miasma of religious torpor—all loomed as threats. Against all of them the apostle admonished, "Beware!"

But in three passages his words come with terrifying power. He seems to speak of a deliberate rejection of the gospel, not just a gradual falling away or neglect. And in all three he issues severe warnings—the sternest in the entire New Testament. The passages are 6:4-6, 10:26-31, and 12:15-17, 25-29. The vigor of expression led to debate over their meaning from the earliest years of the church, and they often trouble Christians today. We must give some attention to them.

How can the apostle couple talk of "absolute confidence" in such ringing terms—unsurpassed in the New Testament—with such severe words—also unsurpassed in the New Testament? How does the presence of such warnings qualify our understanding of the nature of the absolute confidence he has set out?

Undoubtedly the first severe warning, 6:4-6, has received the most study. "For it is impossbile to restore again to repentance those who have once been enlightened, who have tasted the heavenly gift, and have become partakers of the Holy Spirit, and have tasted the goodness of the word of God and the powers of the age to come, if they then commit apostasy, since they crucify the Son of God on their own account and hold him up to contempt."

Its theology caused dissensions in the church of the first four centuries. When Christians whose faith had wavered during a wave of persecution sought readmission to the fellowship, many congregations refused them on the basis of the above passage. Not a few people put off their baptism until their deathbed so they could not fall into unforgivable sin. A second-century writing, quite influential in its own circle, *The Shepherd of Hermas,* sought to modify the apparent intent of 6:4-6 by allowing one—but only one—sin after baptism. For Tertullian, sexual sin lay behind the apostle's words here.

Exegetes still have a hard time with the statement. They argue that "impossible" means "difficult" (but the Greek indicates *impossible!*); or that restored apostates cannot recover the initial glow of Christian experience (possibly correct, but the text indicates restoration "to repentance"); or that it is impossible to restore apostates to repentance while they are crucifying the Son of God afresh (but that would be so obvious that the warning would lose its sting); or that the people he refers to were not really converted in the first place (but they were "partakers, . . . and have tasted").[8]

All efforts to deal with the passage have proved unsatisfactory. They explain it away rather than clarify it. Instead, we have three considerations to suggest. They come with all the greater force in light of our studies thus far into Hebrews.

First, the apostle is not here attempting a treatise on the

"unpardonable sin." He writes homiletically, not theologically. We notice that 6:4-6 comes squarely in the middle of a practical digression from his exposition of Jesus as our High Priest (the digression runs from 5:11 to 6:20). Not that theology is incidental in homiletics—the latter must always proceed from a base in theology—but the insight gives us a grasp of the *nature* of the passage. Consequently, we should beware lest we press its points too far.

The second consideration grows out of the first. At 6:9 the apostle says, "Though we speak thus, yet in your case, beloved, we feel sure of better things that belong to salvation." That is, the severe words of 6:4-6 describe a *theoretical possibility* rather than an actual spiritual condition.

But we still must deal with his words—what do they mean, even if we allow that they come only as a homiletical admonition? I suggest that as a third insight we should not study them alone. The stern warnings of 10:26-31 and 12:15-17, 25-29 are obviously parallel. Unfortunately we often treat 6:4-6 in isolation—it has received a disproportionate amount of attention, the other passages being passed by lightly.

Let us set out the leading ideas of the three passages. We then will see clearly their close relation. Perhaps we will then begin to understand the rationale behind such severe warnings:

Privileges:
6:4-6: enlightened, tasted heavenly gift, partakers of Holy
     Spirit, tasted word of God, coming age
10:26-31: knowledge of the truth
12:15-17, 25-29: the birthright, the Heavenly One
Offense:
6:4-6: commit apostasy
10:26-31: sin deliberately
12:15-17, 25-29: despise the birthright, refuse to hear
Result:
6:4-6: impossible to restore to repentance
10:26-31: no longer a sacrifice for sins
12:15-17, 25-29: no chance to repent, no chance to escape

Prospect of Judgment:
6:4-6: curse, burning (see verses 7, 8)
10:26-31: "fearful prospect of judgment"; worse punishment than the violators of Moses' law; "the hands of the living God"
12:15-17, 25-29: rejection, "consuming fire"
Reasons for the Divine Rejection:
6:4-6: "since they crucify the Son of God on their own account and hold him up to contempt"
10:26-31: "spurned the Son of God, . . . profaned the blood of the covenant, . . . outraged the Spirit of grace"
12:15-17, 25-29: "irreligious," . . . rejecting "him who warns from heaven"

As we look over the passages we observe that the emphasis merely shifts from passage to passage. Whereas 6:4-6 accents the religious privileges of those who may commit apostasy, 10:26-31 dwells on their fearful judgment, while 12:15-17, 25-29 underscores the impossibility of their spiritual rehabilitation. The religious profile is similar for all three passages, however.

Of the five categories we outlined above, the second and final ones are most significant. We see, in the first case, the *nature* of the offense. The apostle describes acts of wanton rejection, of overt defiance of Jesus as Lord. No suggestion of a sin of omission or weakness here (in 12:1 he speaks of "sin which clings so closely," which we must lay aside), no portrayal of the life of the concerned Christian as he wrestles with what Romans 7:24 terms "this body of death." Instead, we have a picture of a man or woman who has known the joy and sweetness of new life in the Saviour but who chooses to openly repudiate Him.

Such a person is guilty of sacrilege. As the fifth category shows, he despises what is most precious—and that after experiencing its benefits. If there exists one object in the course of mankind's history to which we may point as the source of hope and healing, it is the cross. To have known personally its saving power and then to reject it—how heinous! Such individuals take the place of those who actually crucified Jesus, cast scorn on the blood that sets us apart for God in the new covenant, outrage the Spirit, and treat the holy as the profane. It is the most colossal distortion of values imaginable.

We note the apostle's thrust on *knowing, deliberate, open* repudiation of Jesus and His cross. If we could put ourselves back into that world of the first century—his world—we might better catch his concern. Then Christendom did not exist. Christians belonged to a small, obscure sect, barely noticed among the popular religions of the day. The claims of Christians centered in a carpenter who was crucified—and so constituted a joke to both Jews and Greeks. In the face of public scorn, Christians repudiated the popular deities and owned but One as their Lord—that same Jesus.[9] In His cross they found forgiveness and hope.

In such an environment imagine the offense of a Christian's public rejection of Christ. He would not merely signal his change of religion—he would trumpet to the pagan society a repudiation of the cross.

In fact, in non-Christian lands even today similar temptations lie close at hand. We who have grown up in the West can scarcely comprehend the personal and social pressures upon converts to Christianity in so-called "heathen" lands. For instance, some societies make determined efforts to win Christians back to the traditional, popular religion, and they hold public celebrations to mark each success.

The severe warnings of Hebrews, therefore, had peculiar force in their own day. They are nonetheless meaningful to us today, even with our Western freedom and heritage. For is not Christendom itself disintegrating—if indeed it is not already passé? More and more our society turns toward the new paganism of secularity. The myth of the self-sufficient man attracts new converts.[10] Biblical religion is dying out from the culture. And we encounter more and more ex-Christians, *post*-Christians. Some are vocal in their repudiation of the Lord, casting scorn on the religion in which they once rejoiced.

Now we can see why the Book of Hebrews contains such stern words. Because Hebrews exalts the cross in such glowing

147

terms, because it shows so emphatically its superlative worth, it must point out the horror of a deliberate rejection. " 'Every one to whom much is given, of him will much be required,' " said Jesus (Luke 12:48). Correspondingly, that which brings in its train the greatest privileges, even thoroughgoing dealing with the sin problem, must contain the severest warnings to the knowing despiser.

Absolute confidence, then, is *serious,* is conscious of the worth of that on which it rests—Jesus as Sacrifice and High Priest. It does not serve out of fear and trembling lest it fail to please a demanding deity, but it holds high its head in Christian responsibility. Such confidence knows that loyalty is not a dirty word, that it must honor Christ and His cross in all aspects of life.

And so it perseveres. Rather than dwelling on the dire consequences of neglect or rejection of "such a great salvation," it continues to hope and to endure. Absolute confidence lays hold on the invisible world—which is, and so is to come.

We have now explored at some length the great ideas of Hebrews, have seen how the apostle called his hearers, as he would call us, to absolute confidence. Such assurance builds on five unshakable pillars—Sonship, humanity, priesthood, sacrifice, and Lordship over time. And it reveals itself in everyday living by faithfulness and serious awareness of what the profession of Christianity entails.

For a final chapter we shall attempt to look at Hebrews comprehensively. Beyond what we have already discovered, we shall see how the sermon as a whole—theology and exhortations—comes together.

---

[1] We recall the apt description of theology given by Anselm of Canterbury: "faith seeking understanding."

[2] That is, the gospel does not irresistibly bring salvation to all mankind. While Calvary has provided an all-sufficient sacrifice, that provision is to be *individually* appropriated.

[3] It is interesting to compare the other references to Habakkuk 2:3, 4 found in the New Testament—Romans 1:17 and Galatians 3:11. In both the latter the emphasis falls on faith as opposed to human efforts to please God, whereas in Hebrews 10:37, 38 "faith" points to a *way of life* in the world.

[4] That is, humans exercise it. Its source, however, is in God: Romans 10:17; 12:3; Galatians 5:22.

[5] Romans 1:16, 17; 3:19-5:1; 14:23; Galatians 2:15-4:7.

[6] James 2:14-26. This insight helps resolve the conflict between James and Paul.

[7] The classic treatment of the meaning of faith in Hebrews, unfortunately, has not been translated from the German: Erich Grässer, *Der Glaube im Hebräerbrief* (Marburg: N. G. Elwert, 1964).

[8] Some have suggested that the people addressed here have been the recipients of special spiritual blessings, hence the hopelessness of their situation if they reject Christianity. It is not at all clear, however, that such was the case (see below for the listing of their privileges in the three parallel passages).

[9] Note 1 Corinthians 8:5, 6: "For although there may be so-called gods in heaven or on earth—as indeed there are many 'gods' and many 'lords'—yet for us there is one God, the Father, from whom are all things and for whom we exist, and one Lord, Jesus Christ, through whom are all things and through whom we exist."

[10] A lucid article by Gerhart Niemeyer, "The 'Autonomous' Man," *Intercollegiate Review* (Summer, 1974), pp. 131-137, sets out the characteristics of self-sufficient man.

Chapter 8

Christianity As Pilgrimage

The Book of Hebrews is a marvel. It is a *literary* masterpiece. Our studies have shown how skillfully theology supports exhortation, how subtly they merge, how its author introduced, developed, and bound off thoughts, how the argument flows forward in measured, inexorable fashion, how ably it accomplishes his purpose. And it is a *spiritual tour de force*. Hebrews' lofty conceptions of Jesus as Son incarnate, of His once-for-all Sacrifice, of His heavenly ministry on our behalf, ring with a note of assurance unequaled in the New Testament. A manifesto of early Christian religion, it illuminates the privileges and corresponding responsibilities of membership in the new faith.

The apostle has set out a wealth of ideas for our reflection. Cultus, liturgy, Christology, eschatology, cosmology—all invite our further detailed investigation. Small wonder that we so often study Hebrews piecemeal.[1] And yet we desire to take a holistic stance now. We wish to view the sermon as a whole, to see how the rich currents of idea unite. In the earlier chapters of our study we discerned them separately and traced their forward progress. Now we look to discover, if possible, a central concept, an overarching principle that brings together and unites all the material.

Already we have seen its diversity. Its variegated character especially comes into focus in the alternation of theology and exhortation throughout Hebrews.

Consider the views of man and his spiritual needs, for example. The theological sections revolve around a center of priest-temple-sacrifice, and here we saw man's basic problem to be *defilement*. He needs spiritual purification, a purgation that extends to the very consciousness. The Old Testament sacrifices, no matter how many or how often repeated, could not remove the "numinous uneasiness," the continual remembering of sin. But Christ, by one Sacrifice—Himself—has provided forever a decisive purification. So much for the theological portions of Hebrews. When we turn to the admonitions, however, the picture suddenly changes. Throughout chapters 3, 4, 6 and 11 to 13 we discover the problem is not defilement but unfaithfulness, and the book calls for *pistis*—an enduring, patient faith.

Likewise with eschatology. In the cultic parts of Hebrews, the accent falls heavily on *what Christ has done*. Over and over the apostle comes back to Calvary and its all-sufficient benefits. The cross made access to God available, broke down barriers, opened the way for man to boldly approach the presence of God. Yet in the exhortations the mood shifts. Whereas the priestly theology dwells on the "already" and the "now" of salvation, here we encounter the "not yet." The One who came once to deal with sin will come again. He sits enthroned, but His rule is yet to be universally acknowledged. And Christians have no continuing city here. They look for a heavenly homeland in the real, invisible order.

Even the Christology of Hebrews seems to show different aspects as we move from theology to admonition. Its dominant idea, so carefully presented and strongly argued throughout the theological development, is Jesus as High Priest. Undoubtedly, here we have the ruling Christological conception of Hebrews. Hints, appear, however, of an alternate idea. In two places (2:10; 12:2) the apostle calls Jesus the Pioneer, Leader, or Pathfinder, and in a third he describes Him as Forerunner (6:19, 20). While the apostle's "Leader" Christology, brief as it is, does not inherently oppose the conception of Jesus as Heavenly High Priest (Jesus opens the way into the presence of God), it certainly stands apart as an independent theological idea.

Our holistic understanding of Hebrews should be alert to such distinctions. It should be able to account for the ebb and flow of conceptions from cultus to exhortation. Can we then locate an overarching principle that will embrace convincingly the overall data of Hebrews?

I believe that we can. The *pilgrim* motif acts as the organizing idea of Hebrews. In his sermon the apostle uses Christianity as a pilgrimage for his ruling conception. When we see this point and give it due weight, the various materials of Hebrews, theological and admonitory, together with their alternating use, fall easily into place.

We must spend a few moments examining precisely what we mean by "pilgrimage" in Hebrews.

The Four Marks of Pilgrimage

Pilgrimage is one of those words out of the past that means less and less to Western man. Our modern concept is a vague amalgam of *Pilgrim Fathers, Canterbury Tales,* and *Pilgrim's Progress.* How inexact the term is today we can see by the wide-ranging definitions listed in *Webster's Third New International Dictionary of the English Language Unabridged:* "A journey of a pilgrim; esp: one to a shrine or a sacred place . . . the act of making such a journey . . . a trip taken to visit a place of historic or sentimental interest or to participate in a specific event or for a definite purpose . . . the course of life on earth . . . a particular part of the life course of an individual . . . a search for mental and spiritual values."

Such a bland, generalized view of pilgrimage offers little help to us. We need to get back to the fundamental *religious* idea in pilgrimage. Our secular twentieth century has lost that idea or so compromised it that we no longer can describe a pilgrim with clarity. In Hebrews we deal with a religious document, one far removed from our modern scientific age. And do we not even yet sing the old hymns, "Guide me, O Thou great Jehovah! *Pilgrim through this barren land*," "O happy band of pilgrims," and "I'm a pilgrim, and I'm a stranger"? What conception do such words seek to convey?

Fortunately, H. B. Partin in a recent PhD dissertation[2] has made an extensive study of the religious phenomenon of pilgrimage. He has shown that pilgrimage has four distinctive characteristics—separation, place, purpose, and hardship.

First, pilgrimage entails a separation, a leaving home. The pilgrim enters upon a new phase of activity—he cuts himself off from ordinary affairs to embark upon a spiritual quest. He is in transition, calling for an appropriate ceremony. In some cultures the departure for pilgrimage resembles funerary rites.

Second, pilgrimage involves a journey to a sacred *place*. The mere act of religious wandering in itself does not constitute pilgrimage—a sadhu is not a pilgrim. Whether Banaras, Mecca, or some other, the sacred place beckons the pilgrim. It is the center of his cosmos, the navel of the earth, the place par excellence because it orientates all other space and is therefore qualitatively different. It is the point nearest to deity.

Third, one makes pilgrimage for a fixed *purpose*. The human predicament surfaces here. Man in his existential unease seeks purification or forgiveness of his sins, attempts in some way to approach deity. Purpose and place are linked—the sacred place provides a purifying bath (as at Banaras) or constitutes the Muslim pilgrim a haji for the rest of his life (the term actually becomes attached to his name).

Finally, pilgrimage involves *hardship*. The devotee travels long distances, faces physical difficulties and religious trials. The threat of failure looms as a grim possibility.

Partin's study gives us a sharp image of pilgrimage as a religious phenomenon. His four marks rule out generalized understandings of the term. Going to church cannot qualify as pilgrimage, despite common usage, since it does not involve separation or hardship. Even a visit to Canterbury or Rome falls short, due to lack of deep religious purpose and hardship.

Let us now test the Christianity of Hebrews for the four features.

Hebrews and Pilgrimage

The idea of having left home (separation) is strong in Hebrews. God's people do not dwell on "that land from which they had gone out" (11:15); they have been "washed" (6:2; 10:22); they *were* "enlightened" (6:4); they "endured a hard struggle" (10:32) after joining the community. The apostle draws a heavy line between the people of God and "the world." The former were separated, never to return, as they seek "a better country" (11:16). The setting apart of God's followers is not a physical one. They do not dwell in conventicles, apart from the world of men. Rather, their separation is a *religious* one.

Nor are their journeyings aimless wanderings. They have eyes fixed on "the city which has foundations, whose builder and maker is God" (11:10). They travel to the "real" city, for it is invisible. It *is,* so it is therefore "to come" (11:16; 13:14). And it is not merely a city, but God's city. So it is the place par excellence, the place of the heavenly sanctuary where Jesus Christ is High Priest "at the right hand of the Majesty on high" and where countless angels assemble "in festal gathering" (11;10, 16; 13:14; 1:3; 10:12; 12:22).

The Christians' journeying signifies a dissatisfaction with what is "home" to others, pointing to a translation of values in which one can find the "real"—the supreme value—only beyond the world. The Christian pilgrims seek to attain to the real world, where all is sacred. No matter that Christ's blood has already purified them and that they already enter by faith into the heavenly sanctuary—only by arrival at the sacred place par excellence will they find "rest." That rest finds its high point in the ultimate blessing—they will "see the Lord" (12:14).

But the way is difficult. They face perils, both physical and spiritual. Sin beckons to erode faith and faithfulness. The way at times is a struggle. Even martyrdom may mark its ascent (3:12-18;

154

5:11–6:12; 10:23-26; 12:4). The pilgrim may grow weary. False teachings may lead him astray, he may gradually fall back from the group in its onward progress. Or worse still, he may decide that the pilgrim way is not for him and by a deliberate act of rejection sever his connection with the band of wanderers. The difficulty of the way should not cause surprise; indeed, it is *characteristic* of the pilgrim's journey.

Such ideas are already well familiar to us from our earlier investigation of Hebrews. They show that our document does meet all the tests established by Partin. Hebrews does view Christianity as pilgrimage.

We may now be able to see more clearly the interrelation between theology and exhortation in Hebrews. The apostle sees the Hebrews as a *religious community on the move*. Each of the two aspects is vital—(1) they are a religious community, and (2) they are traveling toward the sacred place.

The "separation" idea is so prevalent because Hebrews sets out Christianity as religious community. Christians are holy, sanctified, perfected, cleansed, purified[3]—all terms associated with the sanctuary and its services. They *are* God's people, even now. Now they are "clean," now have access to God, now have consciences purged, now have Jesus as Heavenly High Priest.

But they are also on the march. Although already consecrated and separated, they seek the center of the universe, the very (actually realized) presence of God. The way is long, beset with hazards. They face the real possibility of failure.

Thus, the anthropology of Hebrews comes into view. The defilement-purification conception looks back to their past separation from the world and highlights their present status before God as Christians. The unbelief-faith concern, however, looks to the future, with particular awareness of the perils in the present that may cost them the goal. One may not merely fail to attain the promised "rest," but he may also fall away from the religious community.

The eschatology of the pamphlet likewise emerges into the light. The pilgrim way has three stages: separation, transition, incorporation.[4] The first involves rites of leave-taking, as we noticed above. The second entails rites along the way, obligatory for the pilgrim band. Incorporation concerns rites at the sacred place itself. Any pilgrimage embraces the three stages. For the Book of Hebrews they correspond precisely with the three time aspects: the past, present, and future, respectively:

Then (past)	separation (baptism, persecution)
Now (present)	transition (journeying, faith)
Not yet (future)	incorporation (attainment of the city, see God)

That is, the eschatology of Hebrews is a pilgrim's eschatology. A cultic community on the march looks *back* to its separation from the world as it enters upon pilgrimage. The Christians of Hebrews can look back to their initiation into the people of God, His consecrated ones, and to the Sacrifice of Calvary, which made it possible. The pilgrim community also looks to the *present,* to its current status, privileges, and obligations as it moves toward the sacred place. So God's people in Hebrews, sins purged, even now have access to God and to a Heavenly High Priest as they journey toward the "real" city. Finally, they will reach their goal. To this they eagerly look forward. Then their transitional period, their wandering phase between separation from the world and incorporation into religious bliss, will end. Arriving at the sacred place, they will achieve their hearts' desires. And in terms of the Book of Hebrews, Christians enter into "rest," "the city," the "homeland," the "better country." They "see the Lord."[5]

So with Christology. Because Jesus is High Priest, He is able to separate a people from the world, to set them apart as a religious community in His name. His once-for-all Act on Calvary provides the basis for their status for all time. And even now, as the religious community continues to move toward its long-awaited goal, He encourages them with the thought that they have a sympathetic mediator, one who lives to make intercession for them. But Jesus is more than High Priest. If His priestly function

156

enables the formation and maintenance of the religious
community, His role as leader guarantees its ultimate success.
Because He Himself has passed over the way, suffered, endured,
and attained the goal, He has become a pioneer for the pilgrim
people of God.

The Muslim pilgrimage to Mecca, the hajj, provides a close
analogy. Each step on the hajj (so Islam believes) Muhammad
himself initially traversed. The Muslim pilgrims recapitulate his
actions and words.[6] So the Christians of Hebrews, also pilgrims,
keep their gaze fixed on Jesus, the victorious Pathfinder of their
way.[7]

Although our insight into the Christianity of Hebrews is a
simple one, it has profound implications.[8] With it the centuries
roll away, and we catch a glimpse into the self-understanding of
the early Christians. Seeing them, we also view ourselves in a
new light. It forces us to reflect upon our own understanding of
existence, our own view of the essence of Christianity.

Two questions confront us with special acuteness. "Are you
aware of *who* you are?" we hear the apostle asking. He
challenges us to sense anew the meaning of a pilgrim community
as one *separated,* one that has taken its leave and set out on the
journey to the heavenly city, never to turn back, never to return.
The apostle calls us to see that we are a *cultic* community, i.e.,
one consecrated to God, one for whom God is to be first and last
and best in all things. Reminding us of our privileges, of the
surpassing worth of our Lord in His person, death, and ministry,
he warns us lest we fall along the way.

For that is his second question: "Do you know that you have
an *eternal destiny*—not only who you are, but where you are
going?" he urgently inquires. He wants to assure us that "the best
is yet to be," that beyond our space-time continuum lies the
invisible, eternal order. That is the real; that is to be our goal. We
are a cultic community but not a static one. As a people we are
on the move—or should be. Pilgrims, we journey toward the most
sacred place in the universe, the presence of God Himself. So we
must keep on. Faithful endurance will win the promised goal.

So, for all its present blessings, in our current life the gospel

157

comes to us as promise. And it has ever been thus, the apostle would tell us. The great men and women of old, he says, "though well attested by their faith, did not receive what was promised, since God had foreseen something better for us, that apart from us they should not be made perfect" (11:39, 40).

Now we may better appreciate the dramatic scene of 12:18-29:

"For you have not come to what may be touched, a blazing fire, and darkness, and gloom, and a tempest, and the sound of a trumpet, and a voice whose words made the hearers entreat that no further messages be spoken to them. For they could not endure the order that was given, 'If even a beast touches the mountain, it shall be stoned.' Indeed, so terrifying was the sight that Moses said, 'I tremble with fear.' But you have come to Mount Zion and to the city of the living God, the heavenly Jerusalem, and to innumerable angels in festal gathering, and to the assembly of the first-born who are enrolled in heaven, and to a judge who is God of all, and to the spirits of just men made perfect, and to Jesus, the mediator of a new covenant, and to the sprinkled blood that speaks more graciously than the blood of Abel.

"See that you do not refuse him who is speaking. For if they did not escape when they refused him who warned them on earth, much less shall we escape if we reject him who warns from heaven. His voice then shook the earth; but now he has promised, 'Yet once more I will shake not only the earth but also the heaven.' This phrase, 'Yet once more,' indicates the removal of what is shaken, as of what has been made, in order that what cannot be shaken may remain. Therefore let us be grateful for receiving a kingdom that cannot be shaken, and thus let us offer to God acceptable worship, with reverence and awe; for our God is a consuming fire."

The description here alludes to the story of Israel standing before God at the foot of Mount Sinai as recorded in Exodus 19. Instead of Sinai, the Christians have come to Mount Zion. Rather than a voice from heaven, the blood of Jesus speaks. No longer a group of tribes, they comprise part of a vast throng that includes

angels in the worship experience of the "real" world. Both
accounts describe a station on the pilgrims' way. For both Old
Testament and New Testament people of God, religion involves a
cultic community, separated from its past, enjoying present
privileges, now worshiping by faith the invisible God. But it is a
community on the move, bound toward its future rest, where the
privileges of the now time will give way to eternal bliss.

Thus, we are better able to place the "absolute confidence" of
Hebrews in perspective. We see now more clearly why the
apostle couples it to faith even though it rests on unassailable
foundations. More sharply we discern why he has juxtaposed its
note of ringing assurance with the most solemn warnings of the
New Testament, for the absolute confidence of which the apostle
writes is that of the pilgrim—separated, privileged, but journeying
toward the sacred place in the midst of hardships.

We hope our investigation of Hebrews has succeeded in
laying bare its leading ideas. Trusting that those ideas no longer
loom with such forbidding aspect, we would wish also to have
revealed the progressive unfolding and interlocking of those ideas
in the tightly woven garment that is Hebrews.

Beyond theological illumination, however, we would want
the *practical* message of Hebrews to encourage, inspire, and warn
the reader. If we see only the theology, great as it is, surely we
will not have met the apostle's purpose. He wrote to build up the
early Christians, to place their religion in such a context as would
help them to marvel at its splendor and to determine to persevere
in it, no matter how difficult the way. And may we today see
anew from his writing the greatness and glory of Christianity, may
we see how magnificent are our privileges and what we *are* as
God's people. Then we may know how we should act in a
corresponding manner.

We did not set out to write a commentary on Hebrews. Our
procedure, however, has brought to light the principal thoughts of
Hebrews, and we have touched on almost every passage of the
book. We have, we hope, with the pilgrimage motif shown how
the work hangs together as a whole.

So an ancient writing has spoken again, as it once did in the first century. It has brought home to us the Word of God, showing how ever fresh it is.

Let us, then, continue to probe its secrets. The Book of Hebrews will continually reward the searcher who digs deep—we have not exhausted its treasures!

But let our friend the apostle have the last word. Can we do better than to hear again his oft-repeated note of assurance?

"Brothers, since the blood of Jesus assures our entrance into the sanctuary by the new and living path he has opened for us through the veil, . . . and since we have a great priest who is over the house of God, let us draw near in utter sincerity and absolute confidence, our hearts sprinkled clean from the evil which lay on our conscience and our bodies washed in pure water. Let us hold unswervingly to our profession which gives us hope, for he who made the promise deserves our trust" (10:19-23, NAB).

---

[1] As I have shown elsewhere, such piecemeal approach to Hebrews has marked its modern study. See my "Issues in the Interpretation of Hebrews," *Andrews University Seminary Studies,* Vol. XV, No. 2, 1977; and my "The Cultus of Hebrews in Twentieth-Century Scholarship," *Expository Times,* LXXXIX, No. 4, January, 1978, pp. 104-108.

[2] H. B. Partin, *The Muslim Pilgrimage: Journey to the Center* (PhD dissertation, University of Chicago, 1967).

[3] Hebrews 3:1; 9:13, 14, 22; 10:1, 2, 14, 22, 29; 13:12.

[4] These are the three stages made famous by Arnold van Gennep, *Rites of Passage* (Chicago: University of Chicago Press, 1960). Pilgrimage *in toto,* in fact, is a rite of passage. In terms of the Book of Hebrews, Christians are in transition from this world to the "real" one.

[5] Hebrews 4:1-11; 11:10, 14, 16; 12:14.

[6] Partin, *The Muslim Pilgrimage.*

[7] See Hebrews 12:1-3.

[8] See also my "The Pilgrimage Motif in the Book of Hebrews," *Journal of Biblical Literature,* Vol. 97, No. 2, June, 1978.

[9] Ellen G. White frequently reflects the ideas of this chapter in her writings. On Christianity as pilgrimage, see, e.g., the following: *Testimonies to the Church,* Vol. 6, p. 452; Vol. 8, pp. 18, 175; *The Adventist Home,* pp. 367, 375; *Life Sketches,* pp. 293, 294; *The Ministry of Healing,* p. 478. Note her use of the example of wandering Israel also: *Patriarchs and Prophets,* pp. 406-432; *Spiritual Gifts,* Vol. 4, Part 1, pp. 38-43; *The Story of Redemption,* pp. 162-169.